KERNELS OF HOPE

Real People, Real Stories

Bob and Gail Kaku

 **MAJESTY**HOUSE®

Kernels of Hope

Published by Majesty House®

Mountain View, CA www.majestyhouse.com

Book cover photograph contributors clockwise: Ruth and Ed Silvoso, Pauline Nishida, Tim Tebow Foundation, Cheryl Ricker, Artem Kurdov, Cheryl Salem, Kamal Saleem, Desiree and Mel Ayres, Nana Nishida, Bryan Marleaux, Ann Ault and Christopher Parkening.

Additional photo contributors on Kernels-of-Hope.com and book trailer include: Mary Allen, Dick Bernal, Paula Bicknell, Creative/Wiki Commons, Dr. Garth Coonce, USAF, William C. Hochberger, Tracy Hsu Jensen, Bob and Gail Kaku, L.T. Kodzo, Rebecca Krusee, John Martino, Ross McCall, Rocco Morelli, NARA, Cyril Nishimoto, Dwan Reed, RRZEicons, Shannon Sakamoto, Jinny Sherman, Josh Sherman, Jennifer Slattery, and Blossom Turner.

Library of Congress Control Number: 2012910447
ISBN 978-0-9799903-2-8

Printed in the United States of America

With my God I can scale a wall.
Psalm 18:29 NIV

FOREWORD

Kernels of Hope: Real People, Real Stories. The tales in this remarkable and encouraging book are not "one day far away" Christian platitudes or mini-sermons telling us what we need to do. They are, instead, heartwarming stories told by people looking back on what God did for them. The situations, challenges, and impossible circumstances faced by each storyteller—and how God miraculously answered each of them—will fill you with hope.

Some of the characters are well-known; most are not. Any of them, or all of them could be you or me. What I enjoy about this book is also one of my favorite things about the Bible. These are not stories of mythological superhumans, but real-life experiences lived out one step at a time by ordinary, imperfect individuals who have exactly the same reactions and fears about life that you and I have.

Over and over you'll find yourself thinking, *That's just like me!*

It's what makes these daily doses of hope so powerful. The testimonies of people like us inevitably give us a hope that we don't usually receive when we hear teachers or preachers telling us what we should believe. It's certainly not wrong to be told we should have hope and put our trust in God. But reading about how God intervened in others' lives gives us more hope than we can muster on our own. The testimonies of people like us increase our faith and hope in God.

Bob and Gail Kaku, longtime friends of mine, have put together a marvelous collection of intimate stories that reveal the noble and not-so-noble parts of our human character. This is humanity in a kaleidoscope. But throughout the pages, we see the constancy of God and His goodness. His power manifests in as many different ways as there are circumstances and needs. In fact, the Lord will be the one character who most sticks with you from the dozens of stories in *Kernels of Hope*.

That's the whole point! People feel utterly hopeless when they can't do anything to fix or change their situations. But when we fix our hope completely on what God can do—not what we can accomplish on our own—everything becomes hopeful again.

Want a jump start on more hope in your life? Read these stories.

~ Daniel A. Brown, PhD, Founder of CTW
ctw.coastlands.org

CONTENTS

Acknowledgments

Kernels of Hope would not have been possible without the team of people who spent countless hours on this project. We appreciate all those who contributed stories and reviewed them.

Our deepest gratitude goes to the critique group leaders, Ethel Herr and Rick Hinz and reviewers: Barbara Kawamoto, Christine Sato, Yuki Suminaga, Ross McCall, Pamela Chang, Paul Tabe, Stephanie Shoquist, Sandra Gutknecht, Ginny Walker, Patsy Oda, Robert Fitch, Allan Cobb, Robert Schaetzle, Tim Iwaki, and Malcolm Toriumi.

We thank all those who critiqued stories and provided wise counsel at the Mount Hermon and ACFW writers conferences: Lynn Vincent, David Kopp, Beth Adams, Karen O'Connor, Joseph Bentz, Rick Acker, Brandilyn Collins, James Scott Bell, B.J. Taylor, Gayle Roper, Kathy Ide and Marcus Goodyear.

We are most grateful to Daniel A. Brown, PhD, who wrote the Foreword and to Kayli Catron for coordinating the effort.

We thank Christopher Parkening for the use of his music on the book trailer and Sharon Devol for coordinating the effort.

We are grateful to our editors and proofreaders: Erin Brown, Christine Sato, Charles Dancak, Pauline Nishida, and Cyril Nishimoto.

We thank our graphic artist, Kristina Szeto, for all her hard work and to Lester Tanaka for assisting with technical issues.

Finally, thanks to everyone who prayed and participated in the birthing this book. Above all, we're grateful to our Lord Jesus Christ, who guided us through the creation process.

๛ 𓅺 ๛

Tebow Time

The doctors almost lost the mother and baby.

An American woman had contracted amoebic dysentery, a life-threatening intestinal infection, while serving as a Baptist missionary in the Philippines with her husband. She went into a coma, and doctors treated her with strong medicines before they discovered she was pregnant with her fifth child.[1]

She came out of the coma and the doctors warned, "We strongly advise you to abort the fetus immediately if you want any chance of saving your life."[2]

"I can't kill my baby."

"It isn't a baby at all but a mass of fetal tissue and will likely be stillborn with devastating disabilities."[3]

The mother refused to have the abortion and spent the last two months of pregnancy in bed, almost losing her baby several times. She realized she might not survive, but in her heart she felt God's indescribable peace and trusted Him. Many people back home in America prayed for their family.

On August 14, 1987, Pam Tebow gave birth to Timothy Richard Tebow. His first name means "honoring God."

The attending physicians couldn't understand how the baby survived and beat all odds.

Yet, the parents knew God gave them a miracle baby.

When Tim was five, he faced another brush with death. He was playing in the water at Jacksonville Beach, Florida when a riptide dragged him out to sea. His brother Peter ran into the water to save him, but the dangerous tide snatched him too. Peter managed to swim out to Tim and hold him up until a lifeguard rescued them.

For several nights, Tim went to bed wondering what if something else happened to him. He wanted to end up in heaven. He had heard his dad talk every day about Bible verses and what Jesus had done for him.

One morning he said to his mom, "I'm ready to receive Jesus and be saved." They went to the couch, and he accepted Christ into his heart. He says this was the most important decision of his life. That afternoon, they celebrated his new birth at Walt Disney World's Epcot.

At six years old, Tim dreamed of becoming an NFL quarterback. Many people believed in him, but others scoffed. "Tim Tebow can't be a high school quarterback, nor is he good enough to get an athletic scholarship. He can't win the Heisman or a national championship. Who would pick him for the first round of the draft?"

Yet, Tim played quarterback in high school and for the University of Florida Gators, which won national championships in 2006 and 2008. He received the Heisman Trophy in 2007. In 2010, the Denver Broncos picked him in the very first round of the NFL draft.

People ask Tim if he considers his life a success due to all his football accomplishments.

"Yes, but it has nothing to do with winning national championships, the Heisman Trophy, or being famous. It has everything to do with a personal relationship with Jesus Christ.[4] God put all these blessings in my life. If you believe, even the unbelievable things can become possible."

When Tim was growing up, his parents forbade him from bragging about himself. If someone asked him about the game or how he played, only then could he answer. But he couldn't volunteer the information.

His mom and dad gave him a dollar if someone complimented him on his character. He quickly focused on character and humility rather than trying to impress people.

His parents also taught their kids to stick up for people who were bullied and to befriend those who were left out. That way they would honor God and show His love to people.

On the football field, Tim is known for dropping down on one knee, bowing his head and praying. It has become a worldwide phenomenon known as *Tebowing*. Some of his fans have even taught their pets to *Tebow*.

In college, he wore antiglare stickers underneath his eyes with Bible verses on them, like Philippians 4:13 and John 3:16. After the Florida Gators won the 2008 NCAA championship, he learned that ninety-four million people did a Google search on John 3:16.

When he played quarterback for the Denver Broncos, he'd talk to his teammates in the huddle. "Let's go out there and give everything we have and honor the Lord. If we go out there for the Lord, it's bigger than any win or loss."[5]

He says, "It's important for me to be a great example for the next generation. If people say, 'There's someone who's trying to live with character, strength and honor,' then I believe I'm having a life of significance and meaning, because I'm affecting people's lives in a positive way."

In the off-season, he brings messages of hope to prisoners and to destitute people on skid row.

In 2010, he founded the Tim Tebow Foundation, a non-profit organization that financially supports a number of worthy programs. He's helping to fulfill the dreams of children with life-threatening diseases, building seventeen Timmy's

Playrooms in hospitals for bringing faith, love, and hope to kids around the world, building a hospital in the Philippines, and helping orphanages house hundreds of abandoned children.

His foundation encourages members to work in their local churches, homeless shelters, soup kitchens, hospitals, orphanages, or anywhere people can be served.

Now he's with the New York Jets. He writes: *I will give it my all, and I'll always be grateful to the Broncos organization for giving me the initial opportunity to fulfill my dream of being a NFL quarterback.*[6]

"God has a special plan for each person," Tim says. "It's our job and goal to follow His plan, regardless of whether you think it's the best way to live. God's plan doesn't always mean it's going to be great or easy or the most fun, but it's going to end up being the best. God bless."

For I know the thoughts that I think toward you, says the LORD, thoughts of peace and not of evil, to give you a future and a hope. (Jeremiah 29:11 NKJV)

~ Bob Kaku

1-3. Adapted from Jim Daly's Interview with Bob and Pam Tebow, Focus on the Family February 8, 2010 and other public sources.

4. Adapted from New York Times article with John Branch and Mary Pilon, March 27, 2012

5. Adapted from "Skip Bayless Interviews Tim Tebow About His Faith," YouTube video, 6:44, televised by ESPN, http://www.youtube.com/watch?v=My_lENfJ26A post by "ESPN1stTake," February 3, 2012.

6. Tim Tebow – excerpt from Facebook post 3/29/2012

Unless otherwise noted, all material is adapted from *Through My Eyes* by Tim Tebow with Nathan Whitaker (New York: HarperCollins, 2011) and additional public sources. Used by permission.

~ 🕊 ~

Rich and Thin

My career as a Hollywood stuntwoman began to soar, but I had difficulty staying thin. I doubled for Catherine Bach, a slim actress, on *The Dukes of Hazzard* television series.

At five feet seven inches tall and fluctuating between 112 and 125 pounds, I constantly struggled to lose weight.

I tried different diets, ran, went days without eating any food—a condition known as anorexia.

Other times I binged, eating huge amounts in one sitting. Then I'd feel guilty and throw it up or take excessive amounts of laxatives and diuretics to rid the excess—a condition known as bulimia.

Before I knew it, I was a full-blown anorexic-bulimic on a slow road to destruction. My blonde hair started to fall out; nails became paper-thin.

Outwardly I carried myself as a happy-go-lucky, bubbly person. No one knew I was insecure and unhappy. No one knew I lived with an alcoholic boyfriend who beat me on a regular basis. No one knew I wanted to die.

One day I said to my boyfriend, "I'm leaving."

"If you leave, I'll kill myself." He shoved his head into a mirror and shattered it. Blood coursed down his face.

Terror paralyzed me. Not seeing a way out, I stayed with him, because I couldn't live with his death on my hands.

The relationship deteriorated, and his suicidal threats grew old. One time when I was packing to escape, he caught me and locked me in a closet.

"I'll kill you if you ever try to leave again!"

Heavy oppression and fear seized me. Although he abused me emotionally and physically, I stayed with him.

Then one day when he was gone, I grabbed my things and fled to my friend's home. I moved from place to place, trying to stay out of his grasp. He hunted me down, pounding on my friends' doors and even breaking into their homes.

Not knowing what to do, I cried out to God, "HELP ME!" The prayer must have worked because he couldn't find me.

Over time my agent got me acting roles. In acting class, my eyes locked on to the man of my dreams.

I called my mom. "I met the man I'm going to marry. Mel is so good-looking, curly blond hair, muscular arms—"

"You're kidding. How long have you been going out?"

"I haven't gone out with him. He's not interested in me."

I couldn't understand why my low-cut, high-on-the-thigh, leopard-skin outfit didn't catch his attention. My getups worked with other men, but they didn't even turn his head.

Nightly I dreamed about him, and in my dreams we were in love. His eyes looked at me in adoration. But when I'd go to class and see him, he'd look the other way.

I don't get it.

As time passed, I learned Mel had been a born-again Christian for the past two years. I found out where he lived and worked.

One day my cousin called out of the blue. "Desiree, do you want to go to church?"

Mel immediately came to my mind. "Where is it located?"

"Westwood."

Mel lives in Westwood. Maybe he goes there. "I'd love to go with you."

I went to church, and my heart skipped a beat when I saw Mel. Beautiful music played, which made me cry. It even felt like God was in that place.

The pastor read from the Bible and talked about Jesus. "Ask Jesus into your heart. Make Him Lord of your life . . ."

I wanted to learn more. After returning home, I cried out to God. "Come into my heart." At that moment, peace filled me.

Shortly after this, Mel began to notice me. Within six weeks, I was not only born again and filled with the Holy Spirit, but married to Mel. My dream came true.

My marriage was wonderful but in some ways very difficult. Mel snacked on food throughout the day and never gained weight. Seeing all that food was a bulimic's nightmare.

If I tell him about my eating disorder, he might leave me.

After a couple of months of worrying about what Mel might think or do, I broke down. "Mel, I have a horrible problem. I've been throwing up my food to keep my weight down. Other days I starve myself."

My fears melted as he looked at me with compassion. "We're going to pray. Go ahead." He waited for me to begin.

Butterflies skittered in my stomach. I knew how to pray only silently—the way I was taught in the Christian Science church. When I became a New Ager, I only knew how to cross my legs and chant. But now, I was a new Christian.

"I don't know how to pray."

"That's okay, Desiree. I'll pray. At the end you can agree."

Mel prayed the most beautiful prayer I had ever heard, and the peace of God filled my heart with hope.

I joined a weekly support group at a local church for people with eating disorders. I shared my struggles with them.

One person said, "You've only had two weeks of abstinence. You don't just become free of this kind of thing."

My thunder was gone. Soon I was bingeing and purging all over again.

When I returned home, I lashed out at Mel in tears. "This faith stuff doesn't work."

"What's wrong?"

"I'm throwing up my food again, and I can't stop."

Mel's eyes shone brightly. "I don't care how many times you slip or fall. God's Word says that Jesus came to set us free and heal us." He picked up his Bible and read some scriptures to me. One verse cut like a scalpel.

"Death and life *are* in the power of the tongue" (Proverbs 18:21 NKJV).

It hit me. All those talks in the support group focused on problems rather than solutions.

As Mel read other verses, life began to fill me, and my head cleared. No longer did I see myself as a helpless victim of this horrible disease. If I fell, I could get back up and continue a walk of victory.

My problem was in my mind where the healing process needed to begin. I started identifying goals and studied scriptures about my self-worth. I dwelled on what God's Word said about me and focused on Him rather than on my problems. The more I did this, the more freedom I experienced. God loved me and found me precious and beautiful to behold.

One day I told Mel about my past relationship with my alcoholic boyfriend.

"Desiree, you need to forgive him."

"Forgive him? You must be kidding!" *Why isn't he siding with me?* I only told Mel so he'd beat him up. But in my newborn spirit, I knew Mel was right.

While running on the beach, I tried to process this new concept. How could I forgive the unforgivable?

Within a few minutes, I came across my ex-boyfriend whom I hadn't seen for years. I somehow knew this was a God thing, and I approached him. "Can we talk?" We chatted awhile, and then I looked him in the eye. "I forgive you for all that you've done to me."

His face turned ashen like a ghost, and he was speechless. The moment I forgave him, overpowering freedom came upon me like a bird being released from a cage.

A few years after that, I came across my ex-boyfriend again. This time Mel was with me, and we had the awesome opportunity of leading him to Christ.

As I continued in my faith, God set me completely free from all of my eating disorders. Had I continued on this destructive path, I could have ended up like singer Karen Carpenter, who died of heart failure caused by anorexia.

Fix your thoughts on what is true, and honorable, and right, and pure, and lovely, and admirable. Think about things that are excellent and worthy of praise. (Philippians 4:8 NLT)

~ Desiree Ayres, author of *God Hunger:*
Breaking Addictions of Anorexia,
Bulimia and Compulsive Eating

~ 🕊 ~

Kamal

When I was four years old, I sat at the kitchen table, and my mom said, "Kamal, one day you will be a martyr, my son. You will die for the sake of Allah and exalt Islam. If you kill a Jew, your hand will light up before the throne of Allah, and the host of heaven will celebrate what you have done."

When I turned seven, my parents sent me to Muslim training camps to learn how to use weapons to engage and kill the enemy. We were also taught cultural *Jihad*, a subtle form of warfare, which involves infiltrating a culture and influencing it toward Islamic beliefs and practices. It's unlike the sword, unlike the rifle; it's the Jihad that will come into your world.

By my twenties, I was called to wage cultural *Jihad* on America. In Islam, liberty, freedom, and monarchy are idols that must be brought down. So the liberty in America is anti-Islam and must be changed. I moved from Lebanon to the Bible Belt, where the strongest of stout Christians lived. I wanted to take on the best, because I was the sword of Islam.

I'm anointed. I'm unique. I'm selected. I'm coming to a country and culture to change it, and I have the power of Allah with me.

In the early 1980s, I entrenched myself in a small

Midwestern town and targeted men from poor neighborhoods to recruit them for the Muslim faith.

One afternoon as I went from one place to another to do recruitment, I had a severe car wreck. I was ejected out of my car, landed on my neck, and broke it in two places. A man came running to me. "Don't worry. We're going to take care of you, and everything's going to be all right."

The ambulance rushed me to the emergency room. The orthopedic surgeon looked at my chart and said, "Son, we are going to take care of you. Everything's going to be all right."

The second day, I woke up in the hospital and the head of physical therapy came and read my chart. He said the same thing, word for word. "We are going to take care of you."

At first, I was frightened by those words, because these men were all Christians. In my world, if they say they're going to take care of you, you'd better run.

The surgeries to repair my broken neck were all successful, but recovery would take weeks. After being discharged from the hospital, I needed someone to care for me while I recuperated. I had no one. My family lived in Lebanon.

The orthopedic surgeon opened up his home to me. His family put me in the choicest room with beautiful things. I became part of their family, and they never treated me like a stranger. They set up a basket with a card that read FOR KAMAL. They put in money to pay my hospital bills. I was overwhelmed with the outpouring of Christian love. As I recovered, I began to help around the house with cooking and cleaning.

Their Israeli friends came to visit. I found myself hugging Jews and cooking for them.

What's happened to me?

When I was able to take care of myself and return to my apartment, the doctor had another surprise for me. He raised his hand and dangled keys. "This is the key to the house, and this is an extra key to your new car. We just want to bless you. You can come anytime you want." He handed me the keys and we hugged each other.

I went to my apartment, where I hadn't been for months. When I stepped inside, the dust was thick. I just had to settle an issue with Allah to know if he's real or not. I shut the door behind me and went straight to the eastern window. I fell on my knees and extended my hands to the heavens and cried out, "Allah, my lord and my king, why have you done such a thing to me? I'm okay with the car wreck. I'm okay with all this, but why did you put me among Christians? I'm confused. These Christians and Jews are good people. There's nothing wrong with them. They don't want to kill us. They're not the kind of people I learned about. Allah, these people have a relationship with their God. They cry out to their God, and He answers them. I want to hear your voice. I want to hear if you love me. If you're real, speak to me."

Guess what Allah said that day? Absolutely nothing.

I opened the closet door and pulled out my gun. Because I questioned my faith, I felt the honorable thing to do was to end my life and clock out. I held the gun to my head and heard a voice.

The voice knew me by name and said, *Kamal! Kamal! Kamal! Why don't you call on the Father of Abraham, Isaac and Jacob?*

I fell on my knees and raised my hands to the heavens, and immediately I cried out with every fiber within me, "God the Father of Abraham, if You are real, would You speak to me? I want to know You."

God the Father of Abraham came to the room and filled it with His glory. His name is Yahweh, the Lord is one. He has holes in His hands. He has holes in His feet. His name is Jesus.

"Who are you, my Lord? Who are you?" I asked.

I Am that I Am.

"I'm a simple man with a simple mind. What is that supposed to mean?"

I am the Alpha, I am the Omega. I am the beginning, I am the end. I am everything that is in between. I have known you before I formed the foundation of the earth. I have loved you before I formed you in your mother's womb. Rise up. Rise up, Kamal. Come. You are my warrior. You are not their warrior.

"My Lord, My Lord, I will live and die for you."

Do not die for me. I died for you so that you may live.

That day, instead of taking my life, I gave it to Jesus. I now have a new mission, and I challenge Muslims to question their alliance to Allah. My heart's desire is to reach out to my brothers and sisters, the 1.5 billion Muslims living out there. They have not tasted the freedom in God.

It's been over twenty years since I left the Islamic faith. Jesus is real, and if you've never experienced Him, and if you think you've got nothing to lose, whether you're a Muslim, non-Muslim, non-Christian, or whatever you are, call on God the Father of Abraham, Isaac, and Jacob and say, "If you are real, speak to me. I want to hear your voice."

"I have also called you by your name; I have given you a title of honor, though you have not known Me. I am the LORD, and there is no other; Besides Me there is no God."
(Isaiah 45:4–5)

~ Kamal Saleem, author of *The Blood of Lambs: A Former Terrorist's Memoir of Death and Redemption*
www.KamalSaleem.com

Hiroshima

August 6, 1945 - Hiroshima, Japan.

A blinding light flashed—*pika*—followed by a thunderous boom—*don*. The ground shook and everything went black.

"It's an air raid! Lie low!"

I pressed my trembling seventeen-year-old body against the kitchen sink and clapped my hands over my ears. Objects flew past me. *Will I be killed?* Hot tears trickled down my face.

I was a Japanese American studying in Japan, trapped in the throes of war. On that fateful August day, I was one of five students chosen to cook for some special guests.

The school building gave way, burying me under rubble. A faint light seeped through the debris. I tried to crawl out when I heard voices above me. "Anyone down there?"

"Help me!" I screamed. I reached for the extended hand offered to me as two classmates dragged me out.

"Annie, your face!"

I touched my face and could taste blood from a missing front tooth. With my glasses broken, I couldn't see well.

We rushed to the dormitory to help other classmates. Yoshida-*sensei*, a teacher, was trying to save a student pinned between two posts. One wrong move could kill her. With the help of two girls and Miss Yoshida, we freed her.

A sharp pain knifed my right elbow. I glanced down at the wound and nearly fainted. It looked like a ripe pomegranate that had burst open. I closed my eyes to steady myself.

Miss Yoshida bandaged my arm with aprons. "Go to the air raid shelter for treatment." She fixed her gaze at the other classmate. "Mariko, go with Annie."

I took a few steps then hesitated. "Mariko, go help the other people who are still trapped. I'll be okay."

She refused, but I kept insisting, so we parted. I stumbled across campus with a *zori* sandal on one foot and nothing on the other. A girl sprinted toward me, her outstretched arms were badly burned with the skin broken. Her eyes showed great pain. I tried to calm her, but she passed me, screaming, "*Mizu* [water]!" I stood teary-eyed and helpless.

In the open courtyard, a teacher lay on her back, face pale, eyes shut. I called out to her. "Kawakami-*sensei*. Kawakami-*sensei*." When she opened her eyes, I let out a deep sigh of relief. I kneeled by her and cradled her. A large gash marred her back and blood ran over her neck.

"Pieces of glass are stuck in my neck." She cried in anguish.

Fear gripped me, and I couldn't touch the shards. I helped her to the air raid shelter, where I laid her under a shady tree. Three girls ran toward us crying. "The whole city has been bombed! What is to become of us?"

I began to feel dizzy. "Look after Kawakami-*sensei*," I said to them. "I'm going to rest inside the shelter."

Inside, the odor of perspiration and burnt flesh nauseated me. People howled and screeched like wild animals. Many cried for water, and medical supplies ran low.

Someone grabbed me from behind. I turned, but I didn't recognize the girl. Her clothing had been blown off, and burns covered two-thirds of her body. She kept calling my name and shouted, "Why don't you answer me?"

Then I recognized her voice—one of the dormitory girls.

"I'm going to die," she snapped. "Do something for me!"

She clung to me and would not let go. I removed my apron, tied it around her, and found a place to set her down.

A moment later someone cried out, "Annie, my head, it hurts. Am I badly injured?"

I turned and Chizue, a classmate, was trying to lift her bloody head. I trembled and bit my lip at the sight of her wound.

"If you meet my mother, tell her I'm safe," she said.

I couldn't reply but only nodded.

Our school nurse called to me. "You must leave at once and get treatment at Ujina."

All who could walk were ordered to go there. I didn't want to leave the people I attended, but after being ordered to go several times, I finally left. I passed heaps of dead bodies piled into a large hole. Fires had broken out across the river and would likely reach our school by the end of the day.

I tiptoed around broken windowpanes and other debris as my right side screamed with scathing pain. I finally reached a first aid station on the way to the port. A sign read: ALL OUT OF MEDICAL SUPPLIES. Every ounce of hope drained from me.

Trudging along the riverbank, I craved water, but it was contaminated. My clothes became damp with sweat from the sweltering heat.

A motorboat pulled up and hope filled me. Soldiers onboard took us to Ujina. When it was my turn for treatment, they hardly washed away the dirt from my arm before putting stitches into my elbow—without anesthetics. I screamed and was severely reprimanded. A little boy next to me endured the pain without a sound, while the doctor sewed thirteen stitches on his leg. I felt ashamed, but it didn't stop me from crying.

A soldier, Yoji, handed me some lukewarm water with disinfectant in it. I wiped blood from my face and hands.

We stayed overnight in the barracks and were each given one blanket. Yoji lent me his, which made a more comfortable bed for my bruised body.

By night, the wounded filled the rooms. I slept between Yukiko, a girl I knew from the dorm, and a woman who was given a slim chance of surviving. Yukiko became delirious and broke out with a high fever. I wished for dawn to break.

"Annie, let's go outdoors for some fresh air," Yoji said.

We strode across a wide field. A red sky from fires hovered over the city. I closed my eyes and shuddered. "What a horrifying day it has been with so many people killed and badly injured." I burst into tears.

"Make every attempt to return home as soon as possible so you can get the proper care," he said.

"But I can't leave Yukiko."

"I promise to look after her."

Returning to the barracks, people were crying hysterically and moaning. Doctors and nurses made their rounds, carrying candles in the dark, tending patient after patient.

People from all places came seeking their kinsmen. Next morning, I took Yukiko's pulse and found it beating fast. Pus oozed out of her severe burns. The other woman sleeping next to me died that morning, along with many others.

"Something's crawling on my arm," Yukiko screamed.

Gently lifting her wrist, I hollered, "Help! I need a doctor. Something white is crawling out of Yukiko's arm."

"She's not the only one with maggots," someone said.

"Annie, go home." Yoji insisted.

After arguing at length, I consented. I took one last look at Yukiko, then boarded the free train, squeezing in beside burned and injured people. Then I caught a ferry and arrived home in Komatsu, only to hear Mother had left by boat that morning to search for me. I went to my cousin's home a few blocks away. Sleep didn't come easily. Tormented faces of friends haunted me.

Mother returned home after learning my whereabouts. The whole neighborhood welcomed me as I ran into her arms.

The atomic bomb had exploded 1½ miles from my school. Over 1,000 of my other classmates headed for the open fields. None survived.

Two schoolmates a couple of blocks from ground zero escaped without a scratch. A few weeks later, one of them developed radiation sickness. Her hair began to fall out, and she bled to death in her mother's arms. The other schoolmate also died of radiation within the same week.

After the war, a missionary at my school, Aoyama Gakuin, began to teach me Bible stories that recounted Jesus's love for me—a deep and immeasurable love with no strings attached. It made a lasting impression on me, and I became a Christian.

During my spare time, I taught children at an orphanage—not only English, but also Bible stories and songs that had become a part of my life. I loved working with kids and prayed that I would someday marry and have children of my own.

I moved back to Los Angeles and joined a Japanese Christian church where I taught Sunday school. God answered my prayers, and I married a wonderful Christian man.

Because of my radiation exposure, I worried whether I'd have healthy children. Those prayers were answered, and all my children grew up without any ill effects. I had the special privilege of raising them in the ways of the Lord. Their children also grew up healthy.

God brought new life out of war's terrible destruction. I will forever cherish my love relationship with Him.

We love, because He first loved us. (1 John 4:19)

~ Annie Kanazawa Sueda

Artem

It's high time to tell you what God has done in my life! With great pleasure, I bring you my story.

I came into the world on 08.10.1984 in St. Petersburg, Russia to a twenty-two-year-old Muslim father and a nineteen-year-old "almost" Orthodox mother.

At four-months old, I caught the deadly bacterial infection staphylococcus, which causes diseases of various tissues. If that weren't enough, asthma and allergies attacked my body.

The doctors told my parents, "There's no way Artem will live to see his first birthday. A miracle could happen, but he would be an invalid and suffer mental problems. You're both young and could have another child."

Almost all the time, my home was the hospital. Periodically, when I improved, I'd go home for a week. But the moment my condition worsened, I was back at the hospital, where I'd stay several weeks. The cycle kept repeating itself.

My parents suffered greatly because of me. They tried different doctors, hospitals, medicines, even spiritualists, called "healers" in my country, but nothing worked. Sometimes they saw progress but only for a while, maybe several days. During this time, I used a breathing apparatus, which kept me alive.

Whenever I was rushed to the emergency room, doctors wore hopeless expressions. "Who wants to give Artem the injection this time?" they'd ask one another.

None of them wanted to treat me. They never knew what to do or where to send me, since my body didn't respond to any treatments.

This wasn't a life for my parents or for me.

When I was eight years old, my mother "found" some Christian people. In Russian, it is accurate to say it that way. She constantly sought help for my condition and found what she was looking for.

She invited Jesus into her life and became a born-again Christian. Later she took my younger sister to church. A month after that, she took me. The church people started to pray for me and my healing.

Then the remarkable happened.

I no longer needed a breathing apparatus or any medicine. We had no need to go to the hospital anymore or to see the doctors.

The hospital staff thought I died, because I hadn't shown my face for such a long time.

God healed me through prayer.

Mother said to my father, "You need to get saved through Jesus—God's Son, who died for your sins."

"Don't talk to me about Jesus. I'm a Muslim," he scoffed.

"But Jesus healed Artem! He's the living and true God. Nothing else worked."

My mother and her Christian friends prayed for my father. God began to soften his heart and within a year, he too became a Christian!

After my healing, I was able to play many different sports. I finished high school and music school as a normal kid. I entered the college of foreign languages, and after that, I transferred to the university.

My father used to work as a chemical engineer, but for the past 10 years, he has been serving the Lord as a pastor of a Full Gospel church.

My mother is in charge of the leadership team and mercy care program. They visit people in hospitals, feed the homeless, and help with other special needs.

I praise God that He saved me, healed me, and chose me to fulfill a special purpose.

Interestingly, my name Artem means "healthy and vigorous."

O LORD, you are my God; I will exalt you and praise your name, for in perfect faithfulness you have done marvelous things, things planned long ago. (Isaiah 25:1 NIV)

~ Artem Kurdov

Edge of the Cliff

Dead silence hung between my husband, David, and me like stale, dank air. Each second thickened into what felt like an hour. My breathing quickened then stopped.

"David." I paused and prayed for strength. "I believe you lied to me last night. I'm going to ask again. Were you unfaithful?"

He lowered his glance to the newspaper in front of him. He flicked a look back my way before uneasily turning away.

Tension gripped my heart. Blood rushed hot, screaming through my veins, then cold. My flesh crawled with a clammy layer of sweat as invasive as a scratchy wool blanket on a stifling hot day. I longed for words of denial, or to hear him yell at me for not trusting, anything but this deafening silence.

My mind drifted to an early morning prayer. The Lord had spoken to me. *Rise up my child and pray.*

"You've got to be kidding, Lord. I was up late last night, and You want me to get up and pray?" I stifled a groan and buried my head in the pillow. No, God couldn't be talking to me. I snuggled back into my warm comforter. I felt anything but comfortable.

I had been a Christian too long not to recognize the call.

Quietly slipping from the covers so as not to wake my husband, I crept out of the room. I padded across the living room to the couch and sank into the cushions. "Okay, God, I'm here," I said reluctantly, as I rubbed sleep from my eyes.

Pray for her.

I knew exactly who God meant. She was a longtime employee who had been flirting with my husband. I found some incriminating e-mails, the reason I'd been up late the night before confronting my husband. He assured me nothing more was going on. I informed him I would deal with her myself and put a stop to it. But now God wanted me to pray for *her*. Not exactly what I had in mind. "Really God?"

Again I heard, *Pray for her until you have My heart concerning her.*

I wanted to pray for her about as much as I wanted to swallow poison, but I knew it was fruitless to wrestle with God's wisdom, so I prayed. It surprised me how fast my thinking changed. No longer an enemy, she emerged as a confused, broken woman.

Shocked at the tears that streaked down my face, I heard God whisper. *This could be you. Without My grace and hand on your life, you could be lonely and insecure enough to do anything for attention.*

I rose to make some coffee, thinking my prayers were done. God's next message made my blood turn to ice.

Now pray for David. He is lying to you.

My gut twisted like a monster tornado. Panic touched down. It had taken me hours of intense prayer to finally confront him.

His tormented face now told the truth as the word *yes* slipped from his lips.

"You . . . You . . ." I couldn't even speak. Giant tears rolled down my face. I brushed them off with such anger it felt like I removed a layer of skin. "Not with her! How many times did I question you? And you lied, lied, lied!" My hands flew up in the air, then dropped in defeat. "I'm done. I'm out of here."

Ignoring his pleas to stay, I slammed out the door. The tires squealed as I spun the car out of the driveway. I could barely see through blinding tears.

Now, all I wanted to do was drive my car off the nearest cliff. White knuckled, I gripped the steering wheel. The thought of my children kept me on the road. I shouldn't hurt myself, I rationalized. Instantly, I knew where to head. She would not get away with this.

Never in my life had I felt such sorrow and rage. Where did all my prayers go? Twenty-five years of praying for my husband's return to the Lord, and this was God's answer?

Pulling up to her driveway, I slammed out of the car and marched to her door. I imagined what justice would look like. I could scream out her vileness and let her family know what kind of woman she was. Many ways to make her life miserable danced in my head.

Inconveniently my prayers from earlier that day surfaced in living color, and I once again saw her as Jesus did.

Two scenarios kept vacillating before me in a freak schizophrenic madness: revenge or forgiveness? A battle raged, where forces of good and evil were acutely present. Unsure which would win, I banged loudly.

The door opened. The immediate panic in her eyes spoke volumes. Quickly she stepped onto the porch and shut the door from listening ears within. Without a word spoken, guilt oozed from her being.

You are mine, God whispered into my soul.

Okay, God. That simple admission changed everything.

Unexpected calmness descended on me. God took over. I confronted her with clarity and boldness. She crumpled against the door. Her hands shook as she tried to steady herself.

"I'm not here to condemn you, but to bring you God's

truth." It was as if God Himself spoke through me with His words, His mercy, His grace, His power.

"I forgive you," I said, shocked at my own sincerity.

Tears filled her eyes and spilled down her face.

I placed a tender hand on her arm, as one would a hurting child. "God is waiting for you to come to Him. He loves you and will forgive you."

Disbelief registered on her face.

"God will teach you how to forgive yourself. You were never created to be this kind of woman. This is not His plan for you."

She broke like a piece of ancient pottery. Covering her face with trembling hands, she sobbed. "I've done a lot of bad things in my life, but this . . . I'll never be able to forgive myself." She slumped against the porch beam, seeming to contemplate the ramifications. "When people find out what I've done, it'll kill my mom." Her eyes turned dark and fearful.

"I'm not here for revenge," I reassured her. "Start with God, and He will give you the strength to change. That's the most important thing."

Kind words flowed from my lips, but I knew it wasn't me. God removed the pain, shock, anger, and need for revenge for those few moments on her doorstep.

I suggested we pray as if it was the most natural thing to do, and she nodded in agreement.

"God, bless this woman. Give her a man who will love her like she longs for. Help her to forgive herself. Let her believe that You forgive her, love her, and have a future for her."

Then she prayed for me. "God, help their marriage. Please, don't let it be destroyed because of my sin. Give them many more good years together."

There we stood, two broken women, our arms wrapped tightly around each other, weeping profusely. There were no words, only sorrow—she with hers, and I with mine.

In that moment, I realized that but for the grace of God, I

would have inflicted more pain. I'm so thankful God interceded.

Hours later, when a lot of the pain resurfaced, I thought of that prayer and knew it wasn't me praying those words. The Holy Spirit, coupled with my desire to obey, intervened and led me through.

A few days later, she called me and asked about the God I serve. We met and talked, and she gave her life to Christ.

The road to healing hasn't been an easy path to travel, but moving toward victory never is. Fraught with many months, even years of pain, anger, grief, and sorrow, this sin against our marriage has had many repercussions.

That prayer she prayed on the doorstep has been answered, and our marriage remains intact. My husband has also chosen to turn toward God and seek his own healing. Without his repentance and willingness to change, reconciliation would not have been possible.

It is all because of a gracious, loving Father who pours out His love, grace, healing, and forgiveness upon us.

Only God can take the worst of situations and work something good out of them.

For nothing is impossible with God. (Luke 1:37 NIV)

~ Blossom Turner, author of *Friendly Fire:*
Seven Steps to Healing from Betrayal
blossomturner.com

$\rightsquigarrow \; \mathcal{Y} \; \rightleftharpoons$

Redeemed

To impress people, I did bad things in my life. At thirteen, I started drinking, then began smoking weed, and on to PCP. A relative sold heroin for a prison gang, and the day she gave me some, it was over for me.

Even though I'd hear a little voice inside me say, *You shouldn't do that; it's wrong*, I did it anyway.

When I turned fifteen, my son was born—my pride and joy. I could see myself in him. My family and I moved from San Jose, California, to San Diego.

My wife constantly nagged me. "David, when are you going to get a job? When are you going to stop drinking?"

"Why should I? Just because you stopped . . ." Our relationship grew worse and worse.

One day I left a note on the pillow for my wife: *I can't take your nagging anymore, and I'm leaving to go back to San Jose.* I dropped off my son at my in-law's home. I caught the Greyhound and left San Diego to be with my party friends.

By the time I turned seventeen, I was a full-blown heroin addict, shooting up at least $300 dollars a day.

I was sent to prison at age eighteen and was in and out of there until age thirty-four. When I got out the first time, I met another woman, and we had a baby girl. My curly-haired, large brown-eyed daughter brightened up my life.

I couldn't stop using and knew I would die if I didn't stop. I looked really bad and weighed 135 pounds. To support my drug habit, I pulled an armed robbery and got away with it.

Thinking I could get away a second time, I jumped into my car and drove to rob that same place. This time I got busted.

The judge offered me a plea bargain of four years. The first fourteen days in jail I went through dreadful withdrawals. I couldn't sleep, my nose ran, eyes watered, and body twitched.

During my time in prison, I hung out with prison gangs and incited riots. I also got involved in a stabbing and drug trafficking and ordered inmates to assault others.

Guards took shots at me. Inmates tried to stab me. Bullets from gun towers landed so close, rocks ricocheting from the ground hit my face. In one prison riot, I heard popping sounds from gunners and loud buzzing from the alarms, but nothing happened to me. I often wondered why I was still alive.

When I got out of prison, my daughter was fourteen and had built a wall against me.

I settled down and had another baby girl. Sixteen months later, I got a job working as a cabinet maker.

One day, after returning from dinner, my brother-in-law said to me, "Your mom has been calling for you."

Something was wrong, and the hairs on the back of my neck stood up. Just as he was talking to me, Mom called again.

"David, are you sitting down?"

"No, I'm standing."

"Your son had a car accident."

"Is he okay? What hospital is he in? What room number?"

"He didn't make it."

"Didn't make what?"

"He's dead."

Everything inside me just stopped. I couldn't breathe right. A part of me died with him, and biting tears fell. I remembered holding little David in my arms; he used to smile at me. I always tried to visit him, but his mom wouldn't let me.

Now I can never tell him how much I loved him.

Why did I leave my family to party with my friends? What if I'd stayed? Would the outcome have been different?

My life began to fall apart. I lost my job because I either didn't show up or was late. I started selling drugs and ran around with my old friends from prison. My kids' mom filed for divorce and sought full custody of the kids.

I became homeless and lived on the streets for months. I could have gone to my parents' home, but that would mean I'd have to stop partying. They were strong church people and had raised me in church since I was a baby.

When my drugs ran out, nobody wanted me around. I slept on front porches, even in rain, or stayed in cars.

One day I woke up thinking that I'm better than all this. I went to my parents' house and for the first time, I asked, "Mom, can I stay with you until I get off drugs?"

"Sure!" She lit up.

Two days later I called my wife. "Can you bring the kids over to my parents' home to visit me for the day?"

"No! They ain't going over there, and you'll never see them again." The phone cut off.

I stepped outside and sat on the front step and cried bitterly. I closed my eyes and prayed. A warm feeling came over me. Half of the sickness I was going through vaporized.

When I opened my eyes, my kids and their mom were walking toward me. I couldn't believe what I was seeing.

"David, can you watch the kids?" their mom asked.

"Of course I will."

"Wanna watch them for the weekend?"

"Yeah."

She turned around and took two steps, then turned back. "Do you want them? I wanna do my own thing."

"Yeah, I do."

Wow, this had to be the hand of God! She went to her car and brought me a little bag with only socks, then sped away.

Every night I washed the kids' clothes while they slept. Once I got on welfare I was able to buy them clothes.

Deep inside me, I knew I couldn't live the way I'd been living. Dad had invited me to church whenever I visited. This time I asked, "Dad, can you take me to church?"

His eyes crinkled as if he didn't hear me correctly. "Sure!"

We went to church, and I sought God with an open heart. I used to feel tension at church and always had my guard up. When the altar call was given, something compelled me toward the altar, and I received Jesus into my life. Such freedom came over me—a great release. Happiness and love poured inside me. My addictions to heroin and alcohol vanished in an instant.

A voice inside me said, *Lift up your hands and praise Me.*

"No, that's embarrassing."

If you're embarrassed, I'll be embarrassed with you later.

Bam! My hands flew up, and a heavy weight lifted off my chest. I'd always thought God couldn't love someone like me—a drug addict, gang member, someone in and out of prison.

Reflecting on my life, I realized God was always with me.

He was there when I was shot at and didn't get hit.

He was there when I overdosed on heroin more than once and didn't die.

He was there when on different occasions I had a gun put to my head, and the trigger wasn't pulled.

My two kids received Jesus shortly after me and attend church with me. They used to do poorly in school and cuss a lot. Now they're the exact opposite and get good grades and are respectable. This is the best life I ever had.

On Christmas Eve, a friend gave me a Bible: PRESENTED TO DAVID HERNANDEZ. WELCOME TO THE KINGDOM.

Then one day while sitting at the kitchen table, I heard a voice inside me say: *Barriers will be broken.*

To my amazement just one year later, God's loving hands broke barriers I never dreamed possible. Since last year, I got my cabinet maker job back and received promotions.

The Santa Clara County supervisors presented me with a recognition award for turning my life around and becoming a productive citizen.

Last July I went to Superior Court and brought a copy of my church magazine, which featured my testimony, so the judge could read what God had done for me. More than anything, I wanted the light of Jesus to shine in the courtroom. The judge congratulated me, wished me well, and cleared my entire record of fourteen pages.

Over the years, I began to understand the power of the blood of Jesus, which cleanses me from my sins. He died for me and gave me the opportunity to live a new life for Him.

As of this writing, I've been free from drugs and alcohol for over eleven years.

Today I talk to young kids who are at risk. I believe each of them can be productive people. I also volunteer at the kid's center at church and attend Bible college. My desire is to bring God's Word to as many people as possible.

If God can save someone like me, He can and will do the same for you. All you have to do is receive Him into your life.

Praise the LORD, O my soul, and forget not all his benefits— who forgives all your sins and heals all your diseases, who redeems your life from the pit. (Psalm 103:2–4 NIV)

~ David Hernandez

❧ 🕊 ❧

When Coping Wasn't Enough

My three-year-old daughter, Olivia,* sat alone, banging two toys together and staring off into space. I nudged my husband, Lance.* "What is she doing?"

Lance squatted down by her. "Olivia . . . Olivia."

She turned her head away from him and repeated bits of his dialogue like a trained parrot.

"I have another idea." Lance pretended to fall just inches from her. "Arrgghhh!"

Not once did she look at him.

One day Olivia started walking around the periphery of the living room rug as if she were a toy train on circular tracks.

My heart sank. *What is wrong with her?*

My husband contacted a pediatric specialist who referred us to a distinguished, Stanford University School of Medicine professor and child psychiatrist who specialized in autism.

It scared me. Autism is a neurological disorder that impacts social interaction and communication skills. "Why an autism specialist?"

"The doctor thinks we should rule out autism first."

When we arrived at the clinic, we entered a spacious and tidy office. We peered through the rectangular window and saw a room furnished with a child-sized table, chairs, and toys.

A clinical psychologist greeted us with a warm smile and handed us a stack of forms. "Once you're done with these, I will take Olivia next door and play with her. The psychiatrist will observe our interactions through a video camera. You're welcome to watch through the one-way window."

I squeezed my husband's hand. "This isn't so bad. Olivia should do okay."

After a few hours, the two doctors stepped into the office where we waited. The psychiatrist flipped open her file then looked up. "Based on our data, we believe your daughter has Asperger's syndrome, a form of autism."

Asperger's? No! "Are you sure your finding is accurate?" I fired off in mounting hysteria. "Maybe she didn't test well."

The psychiatrist shook her head. "ADOS is the most reliable tool in diagnosing autism." She pointed to a chart with numbers running across it. "The score your daughter received is based on our findings from today and your observations at home. She has Asperger's. It is best that you accept it."

"Accept it?" Every ounce of my being screamed, *No!*

The psychiatrist pulled out a handout. "Here is a list of support services you may find useful."

On the drive home, I stared out the passenger window in stunned silence. As the scenery passed, so did my dreams for Olivia—big dreams like seeing her float down a church aisle as a glowing bride and having a successful career—little dreams of giggly girlfriends coming over for a sleepover.

In one day, all the longings I had in my heart as a mother burned up and lay in a heap of black ashes.

Waves of heavy depression and anger engulfed me. I lashed out at God. "I don't want more suffering!" I recounted my painful experiences—losing my dad to cancer when I was a child and being infertile for eight long years.

I cut off all ties with moms of normal children. Why focus

on what I no longer had? I struggled to get out of bed each morning. Doing simple things like getting dressed became insurmountable challenges.

One day Lance came home from work early. "I took time off since I'm worried about you."

God used him to help me mend from the hurt and shock.

One evening I picked up the support services list. I shook my head in disappointment. "Did you read the handout? It lists services that teach coping skills. I don't want Olivia to learn to *act* normal. I want her to *be* normal."

"I want her healed too," Lance said.

From then on, our prayers were specific. "God, we don't want Olivia to learn to cope; we desire for her to be healed. Please heal her brain."

Then one day, I received an e-mail for a form of therapy called neurological reorganization. It piqued my interest, and I prayed about it. During prayer, I sensed God speaking to me.

I will heal her.

"How?" The e-mail entered my mind. "You're going to heal her through neurological therapy?" Instantly, peace descended upon me, confirming that I'd understood correctly.

I attended a seminar on neurological reorganization designed for stroke victims. Though it was not touted as beneficial for individuals with autism, I signed up Olivia for an evaluation.

After nearly three hours, I asked the therapist a question that burned in my heart. "Can you cure autism?"

The therapist set her pen down. "No, we can't. But we offer exercises to remove the underlying behaviors that caused your daughter's autism."

Her explanation made sense, and we started right away.

The list of three daily exercises, twenty minutes each, looked simple. She crawled on her stomach, crept on her hands and knees, and performed "cross the brain midline." On paper it looked like the total exercises would require only one hour a day, but in reality they took as long as three hours.

Some days Olivia refused to do them, and she had to be coaxed. Other days, I was more stubborn than her. I'd say, "We can't go to the park unless you finish your exercises."

After six months, we met with Emily, the therapist. When Emily arrived in the waiting room, she said, "Hello!"

Without prompting, Olivia turned from what she was doing and faced her. "Hi, Ms. Emily."

A smile spread across Emily's face as Olivia looked her in the eye and acknowledged her presence. She looked at Olivia adoringly. "Hello, Olivia!"

Olivia's progress gave us renewed hope, and we thanked God for leading us to the right place.

After the reevaluation, Olivia received new exercises. One required her to cross her body with the left arm while lifting her right leg. Others required her to flex her body like a leaping frog or turn her body like a dial on a clock.

We immediately worked the new exercises into Olivia's schedule. Every three months, we returned and received new instructions. Months and years passed, and though we grew weary, we kept doing them. We believed God would somehow heal Olivia through them.

After nearly two and a half years, we returned to Emily for another reevaluation. "Olivia, can you crawl?"

Obediently, she crawled across the floor effortlessly.

Emily clapped her hands. "Beautiful! Can you creep?"

Olivia dropped into a doggy position and crept steadily down the hall.

"Perfect!" After an hour of additional tests, Emily turned to us. "Congratulations! You're all done!"

"We are?" I shrieked, jumping out of my seat.

Emily pumped her fists up. "Yes! No more exercises!"

I scheduled an appointment with another autism expert.

Dr. Randall reviewed the original diagnostic report and scratched his head. "If it weren't for this report, I would never have suspected your daughter of having any form of autism." He arranged for an evaluation with another autism expert. "I want to confirm what I have witnessed."

When we returned, Dr. Randall and a brunette woman greeted us. She introduced herself as Dr. Payton and took Olivia to the playroom with her. Upon returning, she proclaimed, "No autism whatsoever."

"Do you need to see Olivia when she gets older?"

Both doctors laughed. "You don't ever need to return. Olivia has no autism," Dr. Payton replied.

The finality of her words struck me. I thought about all that had passed since Olivia's initial diagnosis.

God healed her!

I had learned so much to trust God's Word over man's words. "Thank You, Jesus for healing Olivia. You are such a great physician."

Some trust in chariots, and some in horses, but we trust in the name of the Lord our God. (Psalm 20:7 NIV)

~ Rachel Liu*

* Names have been changed to protect privacy.

Go Tell It on the Mountain

I'll never forget that day I heard a voice as clearly as someone standing next to me say, *I want you to build a Christian television station in Cincinnati.* The words were spoken calmly but with great and unmistakable force.

Because I was not prone to hearing voices, I scanned the area around me. Nothing like this had ever happened to me before, so I didn't tell anyone. In fact, I tried to shrug it off and forget it ever occurred.

Who was this voice? Was God trying to talk to me? *Why me?* I knew absolutely nothing about television except how to turn on my set and click through the channels.

But two months later, it happened again. It was the same voice and the same message. *I want you to build a Christian television station in Cincinnati.*

I had two choices. I could stick to my cushy life as a businessman in management, finance, and accounting and head for an early retirement. Or I could follow God's call into uncharted waters.

The Lord had been saying to me, *I have chosen you. You have been adopted into My family. You are My son, and I am Your Father.*

I reflected on my relationship with God. He's never failed me. Not once. I took the Lord at His word and acted on His leading. Then I told my wife, Tina, what God was telling me.

"Garth, if that's what the Lord wants us to do, I'm with you 100 percent."

From that moment on, we both made it a top priority in our prayer life. I told some close friends.

"Let's go for it!" one replied.

My close friends and I were just a handful of ordinary people working at regular jobs. We weren't seeking full-time ministry but only trying to follow God's leading the best we knew. Somehow God linked us all together to form a spiritual network before He would establish an electronic one.

I'll never forget the first donation we received. "Garth, you'll never believe it," said my friend Chuck on the phone. "I've just made our first deposit. We got a check for ten dollars."

"Praise God!" we said. You would have thought it was a million dollars.

The Lord spoke to me through a verse:

"Get up into the high mountain; O Jerusalem, you who bring good tidings, lift up your voice with strength, lift it up, be not afraid; say to the cities . . . 'Behold your God!'" (Isaiah 40:9 NKJV)

On Thanksgiving Day of 1976, the Lord said to my spirit, *If you follow My direction, you will look back someday and say, "What a marvelous thing God has done in my life."*

My first phone call to the FCC was quite a learning experience. They told me that starting a television station was impossible. But one thing I knew, the Lord had clearly spoken to me, and I was determined to keep my eye on that goal.

I visited a friend who was in real estate. "We need a forty-acre piece of property on which to build a television tower."

"Where do you want me to look?"

"Right there." I pointed to the spot on the map where the Lord had shown me earlier. From there, the signal would reach Dayton and Cincinnati, Ohio, and Richmond, Indiana—the perfect spot to cover them all.

"Let me see what I can do."

Within twenty-four hours, he returned with a listing on a piece of property exactly where the Lord had shown us. When we received the topography survey, we were amazed to learn that it was the highest point in the whole area. Surely this was the "mountain" from which the Word of the Lord would be powerfully proclaimed.

Then disaster struck. We missed the option renewal date by one day; and the farmer sold the land. We couldn't believe it. Our hearts sank.

We knew we were in a spiritual battle and began to pray vigorously for that land. Within a month, the farmer called us. "Would you like to renew your option?"

"What happened?"

"The man who was going to buy the property couldn't come up with the financing."

God intervened on our behalf.

That same night, God spoke to me through an evangelist, Dick Mills. "I will put a stop gap on the loss of your time, money, and energy, and I will rebuke the devourer for your sake. You shall be satisfied with favor and full of the blessing of the Lord.

"You will have sufficient strength to meet the needs of every day. I will give you My rest. I will deliver you from the constant struggle to attain goals, and you will have freedom to enjoy and relax in green pastures beside quiet waters.

"Your mouth will be filled with laughter and singing. Your neighbors will see what I have done. There are people who need you; I will bless you and you will minister to them."

Even though the FCC had not yet granted our license, we stepped out in faith and dedicated the transmitter tower site to the Lord on July 4, 1978. TCT—Total Christian Television launched its first broadcast programs shortly after.

Next challenge. How were we going to fill 168 hours a week of television programming; and, more important, who in the world would even view the programs?

The still, quiet voice of God spoke to me again. *You put the message out twenty-four hours a day, and I will find My sheep* [viewers]. *You won't have to worry who is watching or who the signal is reaching. Just be faithful, and I will search and find my sheep.*

One night the Lord reminded me of a promise He'd made years earlier. *If you follow My direction, you will look back someday and say, "What a marvelous thing God has done in my life."*

In 1990, the floodgates opened, and TCT entered a time of significant growth.

Today we're a leader in inspirational television with cutting-edge technology and peak performance transmission capability. TCT reaches potentially 1.5 billion viewers worldwide.

This experience has taught me that all God wants is someone who is faithful and willing to respond to His call.

Does the LORD delight in burnt offerings and sacrifices as much as in obeying the voice of the LORD? To obey is better than sacrifice. (1 Samuel 15:22 NIV)

~ Dr. Garth Coonce
www.tct.tv

❧ 🕊 ☙

Out of the Tailspin

Old snow from frozen drifts whipped across the car windshield. Slapping wipers provided a limited view of the Elk Mountain pass.

My friend Geri fidgeted in the front passenger seat as the elevation increased, and I accelerated up the winding, hilly Wyoming terrain. My two girls slept soundly, buckled in the backseat and snuggled with thick blankets and body pillows.

"What's wrong, Geri? I've driven in conditions like this many times over Malad Summit in Idaho, journeys to and from Toronto and Edmonton. We'll be fine." I watched the lines on the side of the road to keep us on track.

My airtight confidence did not ease Geri's fears, so I began to sing "Peace Be Still." I sang the chorus three times before the mountain opened up to the Laramie Valley. The wind stopped blowing. The sky spread out clear and cloudless as the 6:00 a.m. horizon promised a beautiful sunrise. Interstate 80 spanned long and obstacle-free before us. Piles of old snow lined the side of the highway.

We were on our way from Utah to Tennessee for an extended family Christmas gathering, and I had invited Geri to join us. She required medication to keep her mind stable—

something not everyone could appreciate—and I couldn't bear the thought of her spending the holiday alone in the hotel.

Loosening my tight grip on the steering wheel, I moved into the right lane and accelerated to the speed limit. The back wheels pulled quickly to the right. Traction escaped them.

Instinctively I moved my foot off the gas pedal and tried to correct the spin with the steering wheel. But I couldn't regain control on the frictionless surface of black ice.

The car spun around a couple of times on the highway before it slid into the gravel on the soft shoulder. Geri screamed. I gripped the wheel and prayed for control to return.

Instead the right side of the car slammed into a frozen snowbank. We became airborne and rolled down the embankment, side over side. My left leg was sucked out of the door. Each time the car rolled, I felt the full impact of the car or ground against my leg.

Sounds of breaking glass and crunching metal rang in my ears until we landed on our wheels in an isolated, frozen field. Silence fell and cold air compressed my lungs.

The driver's and front passenger doors had crumpled open, while the back doors remained closed. The airbags did not deploy since all the impact hit the sides of the car. Geri crawled out and collapsed into the snow.

Fear seeped into me as the headlights faced the highway, and an occasional truck sped by a couple hundred yards away. "Oh, God, please let someone stop," I pleaded, leaning on the horn.

Everyone was alive, but for how long?

The frame of the car protected our bodies from the collision but offered no protection from the bitter minus six degrees Fahrenheit air that flowed through the open vehicle.

Using both hands, I drew my left leg back into the car and heard something tear. My eleven-year-old, Ariel, climbed out and walked toward the highway for help. Her six-year-old sister, Langston, sat buried under a pile of snow and broken glass. The back window had shattered. I summoned the strength to pull Langston into the seat Geri had vacated.

My glasses no longer sat on my nose, and I was unaware of some cuts on my head that bled profusely down my face. When my children saw me, they both drew back in fear. I'm sure I looked like a scene from a horror movie. "Mommy, please, don't die," they cried. I tried to reassure them.

Then in the soft glow of morning, a man's voice called out, "Hold on, we'll get you out of there." It took twenty minutes for the first ambulance to come four miles from Laramie and rush us to the hospital emergency room.

Geri's right tibia was shattered. Ariel suffered a slight concussion. Langston remained unharmed. Miraculously my leg was not broken, but the torn muscle wouldn't allow me to walk. My head injuries made me too dizzy to leave the hospital.

My parents arrived from Salt Lake City to take the children back home for Christmas. After they rescued some presents from the trunk, my folks reassured me that they'd be back once Geri and I were released in a couple of days.

Ten hours after the accident, I lay on a hospital bed in Laramie and cried. With the children now safe and Geri in a room down the hall singing praise songs to the hospital staff, guilt crept in. It constricted my windpipe as clouds whirled through my brain and torrents fell from my eyes.

Heavy remorse blew through my unstable head. What had I done? I'd never had an accident in my life. Why now? Why did Geri sustain the most injuries? How can wanting to do something nice for someone turn into something so horrible?

As a single mom, I always felt insignificant. I wanted my kids to have a bigger Christmas than just me and them, so I made plans to drive across country to our extended family in Tennessee, where married uncles and aunts could represent to my children what a family should look like.

Tears streamed down my cheeks as I wrestled with guilt. I cried out to God, "Help me understand."

I reflected back on the accident. Black ice comes without a warning and is impossible to see, much less avoid. It's treacherous, and you have no control while sliding on its slippery surface.

The next morning, on Christmas Eve, a day that represents the greatest hope given to man, a feeling of hopelessness crept in, filling the hospital room. Tears fell gently down my bruised and beaten face. Then an overwhelming desire to hear from the Lord replaced loneliness, pain and guilt. Within moments, peace filled me as God reminded me of something.

My children are alive. Geri's alive. I'm still here. Like a gentle breeze, calm blew away clouds of despair.

The nurse tugged a warm blanket over my leg. "I'm so sorry. What a horrible way to spend Christmas."

"For me, this has been the best Christmas ever. I received the best present because we all survived, and no one suffered life-threatening injuries." I paused and drew in a deep breath.

Smoothing the blanket, the nurse said, "The highway patrolman counted more than five complete rotations of your car down the embankment."

"That's truly amazing." I reclined my bed and was filled with awe. "God answered my prayer and sent us Good Samaritans. No one died. This was the greatest gift of all."

God is our refuge and strength, always ready to help in times of trouble. (Psalm 46:1 NLT)

~ L.T Kodzo, author of *Locker 572*

෧ ঌ ৶

Out of the Cataclysm

Full springtime blooms from cherry trees lined the pathway into Shoin, a private girl's high school in Kobe, Japan, where I attended.

Just a few years earlier, Mom had sent my brother and me from Los Angeles to Japan for an education. I was eight and didn't speak any Japanese. By the time I finished grade school, I spoke fluent Japanese and was thrilled to have passed the entrance exam for Shoin.

We lived on the outskirts of Kobe in my grandparents' home, with aunts and uncles.

The culture was different—removing our shoes at home, having no flushing toilets, rinsing off before taking a bath in an *ofuro* heated by wood. Even the clothes were different. Girls touched my fancy dresses and said, "American-san." Or they ran their hand on my mohair sweater and giggled. "*Kuma-san* [bear]," but people welcomed me, and I made friends quickly.

On New Year's Day, we wore kimonos and went to the shrine. "Please give me good grades in school," I prayed to the gods. We played *hanetsuki*, a game like badminton and a card game, *karutatori*. Then we warmed ourselves in the dining room with a ground heater underneath a mat called *kotatsu*. We ate delicious foods for five days. Uncle handed each child an *otoshidama* envelope with money—my happiest day of the year. It was like Christmas, which they didn't celebrate.

Eight months after high school began, the Japanese government officials declared, "It's wartime! Our warplanes attacked Pearl Harbor. All English classes are canceled. You're forbidden from going to the movies."

Instead of high school uniforms, we wore baggy pants called *mompei* with simple tops. In town, ladies were told to dress conservatively—no fancy clothes, especially Western-style, no makeup or hair perms.

For three years, we didn't feel the effects of war until the Americans started bombing major cities. Then we draped black cloths over windows and dimmed lights in our neighborhood to prevent bombers from targeting us. Every backyard had trenches called *bokugo*, which were used as air raid shelters.

The government allocated small amounts of rice to each family every month.

"Grandma, it amazes me to see how you're able to make the rice last the whole month," I said to her in Japanese. She smiled and mixed in *daikon* radish, *nappa* cabbage, and potatoes to make it last.

Soon the government issued another declaration. "All elderly people and children should evacuate to the country."

My heart sank. "Grandma, Grandpa I want to finish high school in the city. I'm going to live with auntie in Miyazaki, but I'll visit you in Sayo-gun whenever I'm near Himeji."

I relocated to Miyazaki, the southeastern coast of Kyushu. Soon after school started, the principal announced, "All classes are canceled. Report to work in your assigned factory."

My classmates and I worked six days a week in a textile factory in Nobeoka, about 70 kilometers north of Miyazaki.

After work, we sang war songs and marched to the dorm. I shared a room with fifteen girls from Miyazaki and slept on the floor. All night long bugs bit me. "Aaah, why am I the only one getting bitten?" I'd scratch myself all night and wake up tired.

We loaded oversized reels of a nylon-like thread onto machines that wove it into a yarn. It was further processed to make *orimono,* a fabric for airplane wings. Each person operated five or six whirring machines at a time. Every time the thread broke, we mended it. We found ourselves constantly rethreading the machines.

When the bell rang for lunch, my closest friends gathered around me, and I let out a broad smile. "I'm so glad to get away from this boring work. My feet hurt from standing."

Day after day, we glared at the watery rice *okaisan* with vegetables and frowned. "Not again. We're malnourished."

My mouth watered for sukiyaki and other foods I'd eaten before the war, like sushi, beef, chicken, and *udon* noodles. My friend wrote a song about the food. Another classmate entertained us with a mocking dance, and several girls joined in.

Rumbling bombers flew at low altitudes as they drew closer and closer to Nobeoka. When the whistling bombs started to fall with deafening blasts, it was pandemonium everywhere.

We fled out of the factory building and jumped into a *bokugo.* Bombs exploded nearby, shaking the ground. Inside the dark *bokugo,* heavy *zukin* hoods packed with cotton protected our heads. We rolled a large *goza* floor mat over the trench opening and stooped down. Machine gunfire peppered all around us. My heart hammered and my body quivered in fear, not knowing whether I'd live or die.

The war grew worse and worse. Once a month, we entered a large auditorium and watched patriotic movies. "Japan's winning the war! We're sinking American ships," government officials told us. "America is losing."

Then why are so many American planes dropping bombs daily? I had heard all of the major cities were bombed. Even my school in Miyazaki.

We graduated high school from the factory with no celebration. I returned to the country where my grandparents were. I contacted my friends in Kobe and planned to visit them.

"Nana-san, don't come. The American planes have been dropping warning notes, telling us to get out of the city—it's going to be bombed tomorrow."

I was in the countryside of Hyogo-ken when the blue sky turned dark gray. "What's happening?" Later we discovered the atomic bomb had dropped on Hiroshima—over 200 kilometers from us. Three days later, another atomic bomb fell on Nagasaki, and the war ended.

So many people had died, including friends and relatives. My heart became heavy and wrenched with grief.

I returned to Kobe and the B-29s had indeed destroyed the city. Shock and dread seized me when I saw the city completely flattened. The sea and mountains, which were once blocked by tall buildings, were now clearly visible.

American soldiers poured into Japan. "Stay out of the city because the GIs will kill you. Move to the country," the government declared over the airwaves.

One day my classmate and I ran into some American soldiers and froze. I trembled in fear, but they turned out to be kind and friendly gentlemen.

Conditions worsened and food became scarce. Homeless people slept on streets, under bridges, or in train stations. Some orphans became shoeshine boys. I wanted to help, but I had very little money.

Many young women who lost everything, including their parents, became *pan-pan* girls—like prostitutes. They dated American soldiers to get food, clothing, and all kinds of things, hoping to marry them, but it rarely happened.

Prices soared in the black market, where you could buy anything if you had money.

Two years after the war, my mom sent money for my brother and me to return home to America. Our two-week voyage aboard an ocean liner had a stopover in Hawaii before docking in San Francisco where Mom picked us up. She had spent almost four years locked up in the internment camps.

My sister stared at my friends and me. "Why are you all dressed the same?" Five of us had bought the same white dresses and matching shoes in Hawaii.

"Oh, I didn't even notice because we're so used to wearing school uniforms."

In Los Angeles, I finished senior high school, and then started college. Several years later, I married and began raising a family. A neighbor and dear friend, Aiko Yoshida, invited me and my family to church.

I learned about the living God, who loved me. I used to think all religions led to heaven, but I discovered the only way there is through Jesus. I eventually became a Christian.

When I reflect back on the war, I see how God protected me from all of those horrible bombings. I'm eternally grateful that I survived and didn't perish.

God has blessed me with many lifelong friends whom I bonded with during my darkest days during the war. I still keep in contact with my high school friends, and whenever I visit them, I hand everyone a Christ Card tract and literature. I also get together with my college friends in America. I believe God helped me survive the war so I could live for Him and lead people to Jesus.

I have made you and I will carry you; I will sustain you and I will rescue you. (Isaiah 46:4b NIV)

~ Nana Nishida

❧ 🕊 ❧

Tea Fire

Smoke wafted through the open window. My friend Becky joked, "Looks like the school is on fire again."

I chortled. "I bet it's the burned food on the grill again."

After a brief silence, we heard someone running in the hall. The suite door of our college dorm burst open. Emerson popped his head in. "The hill's on fire! Evacuate to the gym."

My friends and I stared at one another in shock.

Words flew out my mouth. "Hmm, I should probably bring my guitar and hard drive. Nah, it's probably not serious."

As my friends left, I rushed to the other suites. "Everyone get out. The hill's on fire! Evacuate to the gym." I left my dorm through the winding corridors with only the shirt on my back and sandals on my feet.

Falling ash and smoke stung my face. A bright orange glow no more than half a mile away engulfed the hillside.

Heart pounding, I quickly found myself among fellow students rushing to the gym. I turned around, and the fire had already tripled in size and began to spread exponentially— igniting trees, the lawn, and buildings. *How had the fire spread so quickly? What if the flames engulf us?* My stomach roiled. What if I lost all of my photos? I can't replace them.

At the gym, people coped in different ways—some cried, some embraced friends, others sat on the wood floors and formed prayer circles. Many frantically called loved ones.

I looked up and saw flames right in front of the gym. It was like staring up at an avalanche of fire rushing toward us. Plumes of ash seeped in through the air vents. A group of us ran to the basement and brought up water, food, and mats. I caught a glimpse of the wildfire, now reaching the top of the campus. A bolt of fear shot through me.

"Will," someone called me. "We're going to pray."

I joined the men in my section, and we bowed our heads. "Lord, we plead for help! We desperately need You. We pray for the safety of the fire victims. Be with the firefighters . . ."

After the prayer, an overwhelming sense of God's presence enveloped me. I searched for my friends and located everyone. "Becky. Keith. Courtney. Kat. Kaleb . . ."

In the smoky lobby area, I could hardly see five feet past the exterior glass doors. Outside, flames shot skyward and ate away at the hedges and trees that lined the curb.

A supervisor in an orange vest told everyone, "Don't tell anyone what you've seen. We don't want people to panic."

I returned to the gathering place of my friends and didn't say a word. *Would I have to change schools?*

Courtney leaned toward me and whispered, "Bauder Hall is completely gone. And the prayer chapel is burning to the ground."

I couldn't believe it. The prayer chapel was my special place. I prayed and sought the Lord there for my friends and family, especially Dad, who was going through his third bout with cancer. God answered my prayers there—a place of peace, reassurance, and a place I loved greatly.

Updates were few and far between. Later, the president of Westmont College announced: "We're so grateful no one has been hurt. Some buildings in Clark dorm are ablaze—"

My heart nearly stopped. *Clark ablaze?* If one dorm catches on fire, what would stop it from destroying the others? My nerves went into a high state of alert. How much of my belongings would survive?

Even though I hadn't eaten since noon, I declined the food Sodexho, a major food provider, donated so that more food would be available to those who really needed it.

A few students left campus with family members who made it past roadblocks.

"Will." I turned. It was Kaleb. "I pulled some strings with my boss, and we have seats on a shuttle leaving campus."

"That's great. I'll let the others know." As I waited in line to check out of the gym, I sensed God speaking to me. *Stay and serve those in need.* "Kaleb, you guys go ahead. I feel like I'm supposed to stay here. I'll call you in the morning."

Looking around, distraught faces of those without rides filled the gym. I tried to comfort many of them.

The Red Cross and Reality Carpinteria Church donated blankets, pillows, and cots, which we helped set up and distribute.

The backdoors were opened to let out smoke. I walked outside and a horrific sight greeted me. Fires blazed throughout Montecito and Santa Barbara and glowed brightly against the night sky. The beating drone of helicopters that were dropping water could be heard. I returned to the gym.

Once the lights dimmed, I tried to sleep but couldn't. I rose and talked to a few students here and there. Then I sat down and prayed. I looked at my cell phone clock: 4 a.m. The smoke had grown thicker overnight. As I surveyed the gym, more people began to wake up, and the lights flicked on.

The following morning, the associate dean made an announcement. "Fifteen faculty houses, several dorms, the physics and math buildings, and two Quonset huts have been destroyed." He drew in a deep breath. "Given the strength of the winds and fire, we're amazed that the damage isn't greater. Now for the good news. Most of the important buildings are relatively untouched. The prayer chapel is still standing—"

Wait! What? The firefighters said they saw it burn down. I saw flames all over the lawn near the chapel. How the heck did it survive? I turned and looked at others in disbelief.

Everyone began leaving campus. I contacted my friends, Kaleb and Keith, who picked me up. We managed to get back into our dorm room. What a relief it was to have my photos and see my hard drive and guitar undamaged! I grabbed my things and dashed out.

We drove through campus and observed ruins of buildings that looked like skeletons. Piles of ash, scorched wood and plants littered the campus. I wept silently. "Thank You, Lord, for providing for us and protecting us through it all."

Passing by the chapel, I looked around as bewilderment set in. The associate dean was right. How had the flames stopped at the white picket fence surrounding the chapel? The fire engulfed the other buildings nearby.

I'm a scientist. This doesn't happen. Flames hot enough to melt cars and burn down buildings didn't even singe the chapel fence. What an undeniable act of God!

Through the LORD'S mercies we are not consumed, because His compassions fail not. *They are* new every morning; Great *is* Your faithfulness. (Lamentations 3:22–23 NKJV)

~ William C. Hochberger

The Tea Fire was given that name because it started near the Tea Garden Estate in the hills of Montecito, California, in November 2008.

✒ 🕊 ✒

Free Fall

I wanted to end my life.

After the high tech stock crash in 2001, my company stock price plunged from $70 to $50. An executive in the company suggested, "It's a great time to exercise options and purchase stock to avoid a larger capital gains tax."

With adequate money in my stock account, I didn't have much to worry about, or so I thought.

I acted upon the suggestion and paid over $1 million in taxes to exercise options and purchase shares. Only a few short months later, the unthinkable happened.

The stock market went into a free fall, and the stock price plummeted to less than $10 per share. My stomach twisted into a tight knot as I watched the stock market fluctuate to new lows that I never thought possible. At the same time, I became a victim to a 10,000 employee downsizing.

Our entire life savings of $2 million evaporated just like that.

I went through life thinking this can't be happening. Was I having a bad dream? Every morning I woke up hoping that the dream wasn't true.

My husband, Javid,* and I tried to make up the losses in

the volatile stock market. The more we tried, the more we lost.

Then our CPA delivered worse news. "You owe the government an alternative minimum tax for exercising stock options, roughly $250K."

My heart nearly stopped. "How could this happen? Without a job and no money, how can we ever pay that much to the government?"

We filed our taxes and told the IRS we were going through financial hardship and did not have the money to pay.

A dark, heavy cloud hovered over me. No matter how I saw it, nothing could get us out of this mess.

The IRS filed a lien against our property and garnished my husband's wages. They nearly drained our account, which was hardly anything to begin with, and left us with only $40.

How were we to feed a family of four with two young boys?

I continued looking for a job in the bleak market, but I received no offers. I resorted to selling my expensive jewelry for next to nothing to survive. When I was interviewed for jobs, the people laughed at me because I was so overqualified. They did not know how desperate I was.

I turned to family and friends for help, but they refused. Shell-shocked, I said to my husband, "I don't understand why no one is helping us. I helped my family in their times of crisis. My sister and her husband could have easily borrowed against their home, but they're refusing to help us."

We were willing to put our house up for sale. After talking to a number of real estate agents, we learned housing values had dropped sharply, and the house appraised for only $900K. We owed the bank $1.2 million. Selling the house would mean we would owe the government even more money, since offers came in at only $600K.

We ended up filing for bankruptcy. How could we have gone from having so much to so little?

All kinds of thoughts passed through my head, even the thought of killing myself. I suffered heart palpitations but hid them from my husband.

About that time a friend invited me to a Christian church. I had nothing to lose so I went. As I was praying to God to take my life, He spoke to me. That day I received Christ into my heart and made Him my Lord and Savior. The next week I invited my husband to go to church with me. He had a similar experience and also became a Christian.

We didn't know we could have a personal relationship with God. This was very different from the Muslim religion we grew up in.

A fellow Christian told Javid and me, "Unite your hearts together and pray specifically for your needs." One evening Javid and I joined hands and bowed our heads. "Dear Jesus, I invite Your Spirit to guide our prayer." Tears rolled down my cheeks. "You know I've done everything I possibly can to find a job. I place this into Your hands. You know how much pay we need to survive . . ."

An unexpected peace filled my heart, and I knew God was going to open a door for me. I believed something good would happen.

For two weeks, I sat in my room and didn't look for a job, fully expecting God to do something. Still I couldn't help but pray. "God, if You don't open a door, I don't know what to do."

During this time, a former colleague called me out of the blue from China.

"Azarin,* I heard you're not working. Do you want to work for me at a local office in Silicon Valley?"

"I'd love to!"

On Wednesday I interviewed with the company, and the following Monday, I had the ideal job, which even paid $45K more than my previous one.

I stood in awe of what Jesus did.

A few weeks passed, and I was still struggling with the IRS and going through the bankruptcy process.

My manager who was in town asked, "Azarin, how are you doing? How's the new job?"

"I love my new job. It's perfect." Then my mind drifted to the enormous tax we still owed. Tears welled and my voice cracked. "I've been struggling with a huge tax issue for exercising my stock options. I just cannot understand why I owe the IRS so much on money I did not make."

"Why don't you call my CPA. He might be able to help you reduce your taxes."

I scheduled an appointment with the CPA and told him, "I have no money, but I promise to pay you somehow. Please, please, please help me."

He looked over the tax returns and said, "I could reduce this to $125K, half of what you owe."

My heart did cartwheels. "That's awesome news!"

He redid our taxes and filed an amended return.

I was deeply grateful for what he had done, and I gave him a beautiful gold necklace with matching earrings and a gorgeous Persian rug from Iran as my thank you.

Within two years, our bankruptcy process was taken care of. I also received sizeable bonuses and stock from the new company that helped pay off our debt.

Through this experience, God taught me not to rely on people, but only on Him. He provided for all our needs.

My values began to change as I grew in the faith. Material things became less important, and I valued my newfound friendship with Christ.

During a prayer, I asked my Lord, "Why would you allow me to go through so much suffering when you knew my heart? I had always helped those in need."

Through a vision, the Lord showed me that the house I had

built for myself was made on sand. He wanted to give me a house with a strong, solid foundation, but he had to destroy the man-made tower I was living in.

"Lord, you demonstrated your great power and love for me. Thank you for what you've done."

Since then, God has been sending to me people with similar problems. I try to help them, and the message I give them is: "No storm lasts forever. Look for the green pasture God is going to bring you to. The lessons He teaches you during your distress are priceless."

Today, ten years later, I'm active in my church, and I just completed Bible college. I earnestly desire to follow Jesus all the days of my life.

And the rain fell, and the floods came, and the winds blew and slammed against that house; and yet it did not fall, for it had been founded on the rock. (Matthew 7:25)

~ Azarin Karimi*

* Names have been changed to protect privacy.

Opportunity Knocks

Closing the deal with Mr. Wong would put me in the 100 Percent Club a second time and reward me with a weeklong dream vacation to Hawaii.

Fresh out of college, I joined the tough sales force of a computer company, like a newborn cub without any fear. I worked really hard, and a year later, I became the only woman to join the club, catching the high-tech wave in the economic development of Taiwan.

As I rode the taxi into the industrial district of Taipei, motor scooters skittered between automobiles in bumper-to-bumper traffic. The cab driver blasted his horn at a scooter that zipped past us. A woman holding a young baby sat behind the scooter driver with two more kids holding onto her.

I was confident about signing the letter of intent with Mr. Wong, president of a well-run bicycle manufacturing company. I visualized myself lying on Waikiki Beach when the taxi came to an abrupt halt, jolting me from my reverie. I handed the driver a NT$ 100 bill. "Keep the change and God bless you."

Briefcase in hand, I stepped out of the taxi and approached the security booth of the company. The guard greeted me with a smile. "Mr. Wong is expecting you."

Heading toward the main entrance, I passed between two marble lion statues. The strong scent of burning incense filled my nostrils and nauseated me.

The purchasing manager escorted me to the conference room and handed me a cup of tea. "Ms. Hsu, we've surveyed many computer vendors, but President Wong prefers your company and will announce the decision later today."

"Hurray!" *I knew it. I will win the deal.* The engineers and I had worked day and night for the past month to meet their solution requirements. All that time I'd spent preparing and presenting the proposal finally paid off. The blue sky and white sands of Hawaii popped into my imagination again.

A few minutes later, Mr. Wong stepped into the conference room. He reminded me of a kindhearted grandfather who listened to whatever I said.

I stood up and greeted him. "President Wong, you look so handsome in your blue suit and yellow tie."

He let out a dazzling smile. "Sit down, sit down." Mr. Wong sank into the chair next to me and continued. "After a year-long survey, my team and I have decided to purchase the computer solution from your company. With this solution, my company can achieve a higher level of growth in the coming years."

Holding my breath, I pulled out the letter of intent from my briefcase. My heart raced with excitement.

"To ensure I'm making the right decision," said Mr. Wong, "I want you all to come with me to the Buddha room to burn incense and worship him before we sign the contract."

A cold chill ran down my spine. *I can't do that! I need to find a way to secure the contract somehow.* My head began to spin as if the room turned upside down.

Mr. Wong escorted us into the spacious but stuffy Buddha room filled with burning incense. He proudly showed us his statues. "Each Buddha in the collection reflects a different stage of my life. Some of these are valuable antiques from South Asian countries."

My mind drifted to a Buddhist summer camp I'd attended a year before I became a Christian. I discovered Buddhism is based upon man's philosophy and human efforts, not on a relationship with God and His grace as Christianity is. With Christianity, salvation is one-hundred percent from God and zero percent from man.

An elderly lady passed the burning incense to Mr. Wong. When the incense was passed to me, I hesitated but held it.

"Let's bow to Buddha three times," Mr. Wong said.

My heart pounded as I gazed into the eyes of Buddha. All I had to do was bow. Everything I had worked so hard for was finally within my reach, just three bows away. I felt like I stood on the edge of a cliff. Should I continue or make a U-turn? A verse came to my mind. *You shall have no other gods before Me . . . You shall not bow down to them nor serve them.*

My heart thumped louder and louder.

Everyone bowed except me. They stared at me with bulging eyes. "It's not Buddha's will to purchase from Ms. Hsu's company," the elderly lady said.

I looked at Mr. Wong. "I cannot worship any other gods except my God. I became a Christian back in college and made Jesus my Lord and Savior." I returned the incense to him. "It has been a pleasure working with you and your team these past months." I began to walk out of the room, leaving the contract and dream of Hawaii behind.

On the way out, Mr. Wong said with sad eyes, "Call me, if you change your mind."

"If you would like to learn about my God, feel free to call me too."

My heart grew sad thinking about Buddhists who believe they must earn their way to heaven by living good lives and meditation. With Christianity, salvation is a gift from God for those who trust and follow Him.

Leaving the building, I passed between the marble lions, and my thoughts of Mr. Wong and his Buddhas grew smaller and smaller.

The strong sun beat down on me, and I hailed a cab.

In the following days, neither Mr. Wong nor I called each other. I didn't make my year-end quota, nor did I go to Hawaii.

Later I realized my career had become more important than God. The long hours I spent working had robbed me of my time with Him. I believe the Lord used this incident to wake me up.

Less than a year later, I landed a new job as a product manager with another fast-growing computer company. In my new job, I not only traveled to Hawaii and lay on white sand beaches, but I also traveled to many fascinating countries like Australia, Singapore, Thailand, Egypt, UAE, and Chile.

This job gave me the opportunity to move from Taiwan to the San Francisco Bay Area. Most special of all, I met and married a fine, Christian man through this job.

If I had chosen to bow to Buddha, I wonder where I'd be today. My choice to serve only the Lord led me to all these wonderful blessings.

If you diligently obey the LORD your God, being careful to do all His commandments which I command you today, the LORD your God will set you high above all the nations of the earth. All these blessings will come upon you. (Deuteronomy 28:1–2)

~ Tracy Hsu Jensen

෯ 🕊 ෨

One in a Million

During my career, I made so much money as a world-renowned computer expert, I was set for life. I flew all over the world, including Japan to show the Japanese how to design products to fit the American market. Trade journals featured me in articles as a successful businessman on the fast track.

My wife and four kids wore the finest clothes. I had everything I could want, including my pilot's license and a private plane. But I could never be faithful to my wife.

After sixteen years of marriage, I divorced my wife and married another woman. I made sure my ex-wife and children were well taken care of.

Just three months later, disaster struck.

I don't remember my motorcycle slamming into a hatchback on an interstate bridge going over I-285 in Atlanta, Georgia. At one point I-85 crosses I-285 and included, at that time, three bridges stacked one on top of another.

The collision occurred on the highest bridge during rush hour and ejected me from my bike. I flew airborne over the guardrail and fell three interstate bridges below—a vertical drop of over a hundred feet.

My helmet didn't protect my uncovered face as I skidded

approximately eighteen feet on the asphalt of a busy highway.

My wife later told me she walked past me in the emergency room and didn't recognize me. The neurosurgeon said to her, "Ross's brain has been severely battered on all sides by his skull. Even with brain surgery, he has a slim chance of survival. He may never talk or walk again."

"You have to do something," she told the surgeon.

What was left of me came home after the surgery. I couldn't walk or read or write, nor could I understand radio or television. I could only remember the last one or two syllables of a sentence.

My short-term memory vanished, but my long-term memory remained intact. All I could do was reflect on my past business successes of designing electronic keyboards for standard, programmable calculators and desktop computers, and being the only person who could program payroll calculations from non-gross to gross for the garment and textile industry.

Now I was a vegetable. I could only sit on the couch in the sunken den at home and cry. I vented my frustrations on my family. My three daughters couldn't take it and left at different times to live with their mother. My son stayed with me and my wife and her children until I pointed a gun on them. Then he left to be with his mom. My wife made arrangements to commit me to a mental facility, then left with her children. She had a man, Kelly, take care of me. In two more days, I would be confined for the rest of my life.

While Kelly packed the furniture and belongings, I lay on the kitchen floor wishing I were dead. *If I could just drown in the lake.* The radio played a song I couldn't understand. Then a commercial aired for a revival service at a Pentecostal church. I understood it! I patted my hand on the floor for attention.

Kelly heard the sound and came into the room. I tried to talk, but couldn't. He shook his head and started to leave. I somehow yelled, "Kelly!"

He stopped and turned around.

"I-I want . . . I want to go-go . . . to go to church!"

Kelly took me to the revival. People stopped at my pew and spoke to me. They didn't look at me with scorn or pity. Although I couldn't understand them, I felt loved.

A song played. "No more pain. No more suffering . . ." The lyrics melted me. I heard an inner voice say, *If you will trust Me, these words are true.* I truly felt a connection with Jesus and knew God made a promise to me. What a glorious day that would be! Warmth flowed through my skin. I found myself clapping my hands and raising them toward heaven.

When Kelly brought me home, I became despondent again. All I could think about was being alone in a nut house for the rest of my life. Stuttering, I pleaded, "I-I want to go . . . to go to church to-morrow." I wanted to hear that song again.

The following day at the revival, two men assisted me to the altar. Later I learned Kelly had told the preacher about my condition. The minister looked at me and asked, "Brother Ross, do you believe in the power of prayer?"

I understood him. After thinking about it, I said, "Yeah."

He started praying for me in a gentle, moderate tone. Surprisingly, I understood everything he said. He placed his large hands on my head and squeezed it. *Oww!*

The minister's voice went up two octaves, and my pain grew worse. He shoved my head up and down and uttered words I did not understand. The congregation jumped and shouted. His voice became louder, his grip stronger.

My head throbbed and tears flowed. *God, I know You're real and powerful. I'm hurting. Please, give me relief.*

All of a sudden, a jolt shot through the balls of my feet. Heat rose through my legs and entered my spine. It traveled up to the base of my skull. A bright white light flashed in my eyes, and intense heat shot to the top of my head.

My body became perfectly straight. The fluid around my

eye completely disappeared. All the pain in my head vanished. I jumped up, raised both hands and shouted with joy. "Praise God! I am healed."

Immediately I could walk and talk and understand everything. God healed me through His love, mercy, and grace.

The next day, instead of being taken to the mental ward, I drove myself to the doctor's office. When my doctor saw that I was healed, she kneeled, raised her hands, and wept.

Shortly thereafter, I read *Beyond Defeat* by Dr. James E. Johnson, which turned my world upside down. God convicted me of my general lack of love toward people. I came to the realization that money and power had been my gods.

Although I grew up in church believing in Jesus as a Lord and Savior in my head, I never personally accepted Him as *my* Lord and *my* Savior in my heart. I was headed straight to hell.

I invited Jesus to become Lord and Savior of my life, and His power began to change me. God even delivered me from great prejudices I had toward black people, whom I now love.

I made several attempts to reconcile with my kids. After many years of prayers and tears, I'm very grateful that we're reunited. Also I am friends with both of my ex-wives.

Today I aim toward love in all my dealings with people. I used to think my brilliance got me to my high position and very high income. Now I believe it came from God. I'm filled with deep gratitude and give Him thanks for the miraculous healing.

You may say in your heart, 'My power and the strength of my hand made me this wealth.' But you shall remember the LORD your God, for it is He who is giving you power to make wealth (Deuteronomy 8:17–18)

~ Ross McCall

Double Jeopardy

On a crisp March morning, my two-year-old son, Austin, cuddled next to me by the crackling fireplace. He placed his tiny hand on my slightly pregnant stomach. "Mommy, when is our baby coming out to play?"

I smiled at him. "In six months you will be a big brother." Just then the phone rang. It was my obstetrician, Dr. Kato. *Why is he calling me?*

"Rebecca, I'm sorry to say this, but my colleagues and I found cancer when we reviewed your recent pelvic exam."

My body tensed as I struggled to comprehend what my doctor had just told me.

"I would like you and your husband to come in right away."

I fumbled to put the receiver back on the hook. Had someone opened my chest cavity and taken hold of my heart, and squeezed it as hard as they could? My knees buckled, and I slumped onto the kitchen floor, warm tears staining my maternity blouse.

What happened? I couldn't wrap my mind around what the doctor said. The tears kept coming. With my head against the wall, I looked up to the ceiling and cried out to the Lord, "God, please don't take my baby. You know I just miscarried five short months ago, and it would mean the end of my lifelong dream of having two children."

Randy and I entered the physician's office and waited in solemn silence for the doctor's arrival. I focused my attention on the walls decorated with diplomas and credentials.

My fingers began to tingle, and I looked down to find my hands gripping the chair as if I were white-knuckling a rollercoaster ride. The only sound I could hear was the rhythm of my heartbeat, which seemed to have found its way into my throat. That's when the door opened and Dr. Kato walked in.

The last things I remember hearing were "radiation," "chemotherapy," and "immediately."

This had to be some kind of mistake. The test results couldn't be mine. I gasped for air as reality sank in. The radiation would cause my body to reject my twelve-week-old fetus.

The ride home was a blur. After stepping into our house, Randy reached for our Bible. We drew comfort and strength from our faith in God and from each other's love. We stumbled upon the following verse:

> Are any of you sick? You should call for the elders of the church to come and pray over you, anointing you with oil in the name of the Lord. Such a prayer offered in faith will heal the sick, and the Lord will make you well. And if you have committed any sins, you will be forgiven. (James 5:14–15 NLT)

All week long, Randy lost sleep, tossing and turning throughout the night. He agonized over the possibility of losing me and the baby. He grabbed his pillow each night, hit the couch, and cried out for God to intervene.

Toward the end of the week, it dawned on us. "Maybe God

was speaking to us through the verse." We had to act now. We hurried to meet with our church elders.

One pastor placed anointing oil on my forehead. I counted five other pastors kneeling at my feet and praying to Jesus to heal me of this cancer and protect our baby.

Two weeks later, I received another phone call from Dr. Kato for a follow-up appointment.

What in the world is he going to tell me this time? I could barely stay composed.

"Well," he said, "we've had a change of plans."

"A change of plans? Are they good or bad?" My brain cells braced themselves for the next blow.

"I consulted with my peers, and we decided to surgically remove your cancer. This will allow you to deliver your baby on your due date. Then we will begin your regime."

Tears welled as I choked out the words, "Does this mean I'll be fine, and I get to keep my baby?"

"Yes, it does, Rebecca." Uncontainable joy filled me. If I were a bubble, I would have burst. My tears fell, but this time they were tears of joy.

Days turned to weeks, and weeks turned to months as my belly took on the shape of a small bowling ball.

On the day of my surgery, I lay on a cold, sterile operating table and stared at the ceiling through laser-safety glasses. The brightest white lights I had ever seen illuminated the room. The clinking and clanging of stainless steel medical equipment rattled in the background while the doctors discussed the procedure. My knees quivered uncontrollably for nearly three hours as my thoughts raced laps around my head.

Is my baby going to be okay?

This, by far, was the most difficult thing I had ever gone through. My tense muscles released when it was over.

Two months later, I found myself lying on another operating table for a procedure called "Clear Area," a simple surgery to check whether my cancer was gone.

After the procedure, my doctor gave us the report. "I have great news. All of your cancer is gone! And there's no need for you to undergo any radiation or chemotherapy after your child is born."

My heart did backflips. Randy and I fell into each other's arms. God had just given us our very own modern-day miracle.

In September I gave birth to a healthy, blonde, blue-eyed girl—Alicia Lee Krusee. This beautiful 19-inch-long bundle weighed 6 pounds 12 ounces. Just thirty-nine years earlier, her mother was born with the exact same weight and length.

What an amazing gift from God.

Every good thing given and every perfect gift is from above, coming down from the Father of lights, with whom there is no variation or shifting shadow. (James 1:17)

~ Rebecca Krusee

Break Free

My life turned completely upside down when Mom divorced Dad and married his best friend. I was fifteen years old, the eldest son of three children born in Panama.

How could Mom do that? I hated her. The Catholic church we faithfully attended excommunicated us when Mom divorced. That's when we stopped going to church altogether.

Rage, insecurity, abandonment consumed me. I constantly looked to women to fill the void within me and give me the love I never received as a child. I sought sexual relations to relieve my insecurities. When I turned twenty two, I relocated from Panama to the U.S. to finish my college degree.

In the years that followed, I engaged in many promiscuous relationships with women and became obsessed with sex. I visited strip clubs and buried myself in magazines like *Playboy* and *Penthouse*.

If it's okay for Dad to read these, it's okay for me.

Soon after that, I met my future wife, Dawn, and we married two years later. I immediately became a stepfather to three kids. A few years later, Dawn and I had a child together. I thought I was happy, but I once again fell prey to pornography.

I'm not hurting anyone.

Dawn caught me red-handed. "What? Am I not enough for you? Don't I satisfy you?"

"I promise I'll never do it again."

In the days that followed, that compelling drive wouldn't quit. *Why can't I stop? Why do I feel the need to satisfy my sexual desires outside of my marriage?*

After seven years of marriage, Dawn accepted the Lord as her personal Savior, and soon I followed and my spirit became reborn. Since we both grew up Catholic, this was a new experience for us. My family and I attended church regularly, joined a Bible study group, and I did daily devotions. I also played electric guitar in the worship band.

Ironically, my obsession with sex grew worse. I traveled a lot on my job and caved in to Internet porn. One day God spoke to me through the following verse:

"Let there be no sexual immorality, impurity, or greed among you. Such sins have no place among God's people" (Ephesians 5:3 NLT).

But I succumbed to temptations. I figured I could do these things in secret and not hurt anyone. I wrestled between spiritual forces of evil and the new life Jesus gave me. Soon magazines and Internet porn were not enough, and I sought sexual relations outside my marriage. God spoke to me through another verse, which hit me like a ton of lead:

"When you follow the desires of your sinful nature, the results are very clear: sexual immorality, impurity, lustful pleasure" (Galatians 5:19 NLT).

Guilt, shame, and sorrow bore down on me, yet I could not stop or control myself. Eventually I gave up on my marriage and even on myself. Surely I'd burn in hell for this.

In due course, Dawn figured out I had been sleeping around. She confronted me, and I came clean about everything. I revealed to her the many years of secret sins and infidelity.

She fainted and dropped to the floor. When she came to, she cried and screamed. "How could you do this all these years, you son of a #$@%!"

"Honey, . . . I promise I'll never do it again."

She had heard this before. She couldn't bear it, so she left me and filed for divorce.

Devastated to the core, I bawled for days and pleaded for God's help. "Jesus, my life is unmanageable. I'm powerless over my sins. I'm willing to do anything to restore my relationship with You, Dawn, and my children. I completely surrender to You and submit to Your will. Forgive me of all my sins and cleanse me of my unrighteousness."

Immediately I started attending a local church mainly because of its Christ-centered recovery program that dealt with all types of hurts, habits, and hang-ups. On my first visit, caring people surrounded me, willing to help me overcome my problems. I quickly hooked up with a small support group.

I'm not alone.

Dawn and the children didn't want anything to do with me. But I continued with the program, knowing this was the right thing to do for my own sanity and healing.

The following months were very difficult, but I was determined to overcome this sin. I relied solely on God's strength to get me through each day, one day at a time, moment by moment.

Many times I cried out to Him. "Lord, have mercy on me and send me Your Comforter. I believe You will deliver me and restore my relationships if I'm obedient and faithful to You."

After a long time lapsed, I contacted Dawn. "Please give me a second chance."

After what seemed like an eternity, she responded. "You are to continue working the twelve-step program with a sponsor. Be subject to periodic polygraph tests. Be accountable for your time and money."

For the first time, a renewed hope filled me. This would be my *one and only* opportunity to make things right.

I blew out a deep breath of relief. "Honey, we can do this together, so I'm asking for your support. Please attend the weekly recovery meetings with me."

Dawn met other women at the meetings who were struggling with the same issues. She realized she wasn't alone, and she discussed her fears and insecurities with them.

As I grew stronger in my faith and obeyed God, He poured out many blessings upon our lives, including the restoration of our marriage and my relationship with my children. I learned that my identity was not in my sexual sin but in Jesus Christ.

God replaced my fits of rage, feelings of insecurities and abandonment with His love, wholeness, and inner peace.

Today I am free from the destructive behaviors that had consumed my life for many years. I have turned my back on those sins forever!

It is possible to have love, joy, peace, patience, kindness, goodness, gentleness, faithfulness, and, most important, self control.

All Scripture is God-breathed and is useful for teaching, rebuking, correcting and training in righteousness, so that the man of God may be thoroughly equipped for every good work. (2 Timothy 3:16–17 NIV)

~ John Martino

Cooking Up a Little Faith

The stench of burned pasta filled the kitchen as gray smoke billowed from the oven. I yanked the blackened remains of another meal out of the oven and pitched it through the back door.

The metal pan sizzled and crackled as it hit the snow mound. I groaned and fought back tears of frustration.

In the year my husband, John, and I married, the simple task of cooking had gone from challenging to impossible with an oven that fluctuated between 0 and 550 degrees.

Car lights swung into the driveway, heralding my husband's arrival. The car engine quieted, and for a moment, everything seemed still.

I shivered in the open doorway and coughed as the smoke billowed past me. I couldn't see him in the dark interior of his vehicle, but I imagined he was staring back. The driver's door creaked open. He stepped out of the truck.

"Another supper goes up in smoke," he said, trying to make a joke. "What was it this time?"

"Lasagna."

"Aw, man. You make such great lasagna." He put an arm

around my shoulders as we mourned the loss of our supper.

We went into the little rental house we called home. We flung open the windows and fanned the smoke into the winter night. I dumped a can of chicken soup into a pan and splashed in water.

John frowned at the gaping oven then slammed its door shut. "We'll get a new stove as soon as work picks up." It had become a common refrain.

I nodded. "As soon as work picks up and the truck transmission doesn't go out. Or the tires don't blow on the car or anything goes wrong with this pregnancy."

Wishing, hoping, and planning hadn't gotten us a new stove. I determined to exercise faith.

I had attended church since birth but only came to know Jesus as Savior and Lord the year before we married. Since that time, I'd been taught God hears and answers when you pray specifically. I needed Him to intervene.

The next morning I knelt on the cold linoleum floor and leaned over the seat of the green vinyl rocker. I folded my hands and bowed my head. This was serious business. "God, you see how we've been struggling along with this old stove. We need an oven that works. Please, find us one we can afford."

Later that week, my husband entered the house with a bright smile on his face. "A client has a tenant who is moving and doesn't want to transport the kitchen appliances across country. Do you want to go look at their stove?"

"Let me grab my purse." I ran into the bedroom, snatched my coat, and followed him to the truck.

I'd never seen a nicer model. Four electric burners topped a clean, shiny full-sized stove. It was only a year old and featured delayed cooking, a regular clock with timer, an overhead warming shelf and extra light. Best of all, it worked. Oh, how I wanted that stove. I gave my husband a nod.

"How much?" he asked.

"We're leaving day after tomorrow. We've got to get rid of it. How about eighty dollars?"

We looked at each other and told them we would let them know.

Back in our vehicle, the ride home was quiet. What a perfect stove—but how would we ever get the money?

The next day I received a call from our bank. A woman I didn't know said, "I'm calling to inform you that during a recent audit we discovered a mistake on your account."

My heart pounded and thrashed as it sunk from its usual place in my chest to the pit of my stomach. "We're overdrawn? How could such a thing happen?"

The professional-sounding voice said, "No, ma'am. It's not an overdraft. It's a bank error. Eight months ago you made a deposit that was debited from your account instead of credited. You have eighty dollars more than what your balance currently shows."

I thanked her again and again and sank into the nearby chair, the same chair where I had presented my need to God. My seed of faith moved a mountain. That day trust in God's faithfulness was birthed in my heart.

Cast all your anxiety on him because he cares for you.
(1 Peter 5:7 NIV)

~ Mary Allen, freelance writer

Soli Deo Gloria

For over a quarter century, I have been known in the classical music world as a concert guitarist, following the tradition of the great Spanish guitarist Andrés Segovia.

Before I began playing the guitar, I had a great love of the outdoors. In particular, I loved fly-fishing for trout, which my dad taught me when I was six years old. My goal in life was to someday own my own ranch and private trout stream, make a lot of money, and enjoy the good life. Since my father had retired at forty-seven, I decided thirty would be a good retirement age for me.

I grew up in Los Angeles and started playing the guitar at the age of eleven. My cousin, Jack Marshall, who was the staff guitarist at MGM Studios, inspired me.

"I love the way you play the guitar," I said to him. "I would like to study guitar."

"Christopher, learn the classical technique first to establish solid technical skills. Also purchase the recordings of Andrés Segovia, the greatest guitarist in the world."

The full, rich notes from Segovia's guitar sounded like no other. He impressed me so much that I started classical, loved it, and stayed with it.

My parents taught me the value of hard work and discipline. Father encouraged me to wake up at 5:00 a.m. and practice for an hour and a half before school and again in the afternoon. This created a conflict in me since I had a keen interest in sports.

My hard work began to pay off. At age fifteen, I was invited to attend Andrés Segovia's first United States master class at the University of California at Berkeley.

What a great honor to play for the man who had inspired me for so many years! He told me, "Christopher, you have the potential for a wonderful career with the classical guitar. Work very hard."

It was my good fortune to continue private study with Segovia and later, when I attended the University of Southern California, to study musical interpretation with world renowned cellist Gregor Piatigorsky.

At age nineteen, I signed with Capitol Records for a series of six albums and was asked to start a guitar department at the University of Southern California.

The following year I signed with Columbia Artists Management for a rigorous concert schedule touring the United States, Canada, Europe, and Asia, eventually performing over ninety concerts a year. Needless to say, as I added a grueling concert schedule to my teaching and recording obligations, my life became ever more stressful.

I was miserable on tour and hated hotel rooms, airplanes, and the monotony of one concert after the next. I thought, "There will come a day when I will be happy. I'll have my own ranch with my own trout stream and I can retire. I can do what I want to do, go where I want to go, and be content."

At thirty, I achieved my goal.

I stopped playing the guitar and found a ranch with a beautiful trout stream in Montana and relocated from Southern California. I called Capitol Records, USC, and Columbia

Artists Management to thank them, and to let them know I wouldn't be playing the guitar anymore. I had achieved my life's dream.

For the next four years, I did everything I wanted to do. I fished to my heart's content, learning every trout stream in the area. I'd travel back to Southern California in the winter to escape the snow and cold weather. I was living the good life, or so I thought.

My ideal life was turning out to be not so ideal after all. I became bored and began to feel empty inside. I needed something more; something to provide the fulfillment that my success didn't give me.

During a winter visit to Southern California, a neighbor leaned over the backyard fence and invited me to Grace Community Church. I decided to go.

John MacArthur preached a sermon, "Examine Yourself Whether You Be in the Faith," and he read:

> "Not everyone who says to Me, 'Lord, Lord,' shall enter the kingdom of heaven, but he who does the will of My Father in heaven. Many will say to Me in that day, 'Lord, Lord, have we not prophesied in Your name, cast out demons in Your name, and done many wonders in Your name?' And then I will declare to them, 'I never knew you; depart from Me, you who practice lawlessness!'" Matthew 7:21-23 (NKJV).

As I listened to the words Pastor MacArthur read, something cut deep into my heart. "That's me! I would be one of those who say, 'Lord, Lord, I believe who You are. I went to Sunday school every week when I was a young child. My parents even had me baptized. I read the Bible occasionally.'"

In my heart I knew Jesus would answer me, 'You never cared to glorify Me with your life or with your music. All you cared about were your ranches and your trout streams. Depart from Me, I never knew you!'

In that sudden, terrible moment, I realized I was not a Christian. Because I knew the "facts" about Jesus Christ, I thought I would get into heaven. I had faith, but my lifestyle had been characterized by total selfishness and disobedience. I supposed I had wanted a Savior to save me from hell, but I never wanted a Lord of my life whom I should follow, trust, and obey.

That night I lay awake, broken over my sins. My life was a total washout. I had lived very selfishly, and it didn't make me happy. Knowing I was a sinner before God, I prayed and asked Him to forgive me. It was then that I asked Jesus Christ to come into my life, to be my Lord and Savior. For the first time, I remember telling Him, "Whatever You want me to do with my life, Lord, I'll do it."

My new commitment to Christ gave me a great desire to read the Bible and learn more about the Word of God. One day I read the passage from the Bible:

Whatever you do, do all to the glory of God.
(1 Corinthians 10:31 NKJV)

I only knew how to do two things: fly-fishing and play the guitar. The latter seemed to be the better option to pursue.

The great composer J.S. Bach said, "The aim and final reason of all music is none else but the glory of God." Bach signed many of his compositions with the initials S.D.G., which stands for Soli Deo Gloria [to God alone the glory].

If Bach could use his great ability for that purpose, that would be the least I could do with whatever ability or talent the Lord had given me. It became evident that the Lord wanted me to return to the guitar, but this time with a different purpose— to honor and glorify my Lord and Savior Jesus Christ.

Shortly after making this decision, I sold my ranch in Montana and returned to California.

Initially I had a rude awakening when I contacted my former manager in New York.

He told me flatly, "Christopher, you had thrown away a very valuable career. It would be extremely difficult, if not impossible, to return to the concert stage after a four-year absence."

I knew it would be only by God's grace that I would be able to return to a professional music career.

The Lord has been gracious. Since my return to the music world, I played with every major orchestra in the nation, traveled the world on countless concert tours and even played for the President of the United States at the White House.

Even though I desire to follow Andrés Segovia with excellence and the musical tradition he left us, my true goal in life is to be a good and faithful servant of the Lord Jesus Christ. At concerts I tell my audiences that I take my faith in Jesus very seriously, and I play my music unto Him.

My career is only a means to an end, and that end is to glorify the Lord with my life and the music I play. Pursuing that goal gives me great joy and contentment, and the fulfillment which eluded me so many years ago has been found at last, and the emptiness I once had gone forever.

For what profit is it to a man if he gains the whole world, and loses his own soul? Or what will a man give in exchange for his soul? (Matthew 16:26 NKJV)

~ Christopher Parkening
Distinguished Professor of Music
Pepperdine University, Malibu, California
www.parkening.com

🙐 🕊 🙖

All Shook Up

A thunderous boom like a plane crash and a sharp jolt followed by violent up-and-down shaking thrust me out of bed. I lunged toward the hallway and gripped the doorjamb as the ground beneath my feet dropped and shook like an out-of-control washing machine.

My heart pounded with fear. "Jesus, *heeelp!* Is this the big one? Please, keep us all safe! Will I be buried alive?"

Windows rattled, glass shattered, and all kinds of loud sounds reverberated throughout my townhome. Alarms went off. My stomach twisted and churned. After what seemed like an eternity, the upheaval stopped. I flipped on the light switch—but nothing.

Barefoot, I stepped back into the bedroom, gingerly avoiding shards of glass. *What are those big clumps of wood?* My room looked like a construction zone. "Where are my shoes? My glasses?" I crunched my foot on something. "Ow!" Carefully, I made my way back towards the bathroom. It's a miracle I found my contact lens case that had toppled out of the cabinet into the sink. I popped the lenses into my tired eyes.

After a scavenger hunt, I found my glasses in one piece. I scoured around, found shoes and slid my feet into them.

Later it dawned on me: those big clumps of wood were my dresser drawers flipped upside down. *How did they fly across the pathway from my bed to the doorway without hitting me?*

Earlier that morning, I tossed and turned into the wee hours. *Okay, Lord, You must want me to pray for someone.* In the midst of praying, the quake hit. *I should've been praying for everyone.* Thank God, I was already awake, so I could move faster than the flying drawers.

Bolting downstairs to the kitchen area, adrenaline pumped through my veins as I surveyed the disarray. "What a mess!" Cupboards hung open, emptied. Food from the refrigerator and freezer was strewn across the floor, mingled with frozen Tupperware cracked open and broken dishes.

Venturing outside, I checked on my neighbors. Thank God, no one was injured!

I kept wondering whether Mom and Dad were safe. With the power outage, how would I get my car out through the security gate to get to my parents? Then I remembered the gate broke the night before and was left wide open.

Driving the few miles to my parents' home was a great challenge, dodging piles of rubble and deep cracks in the roadway like an obstacle course. Nearby homes were tilted over, but my parents' house stood upright.

Mom and Dad were waiting for me at the door. "Boy, the house shook for the longest time," Mom said. "I'm surprised it's still standing. We didn't get hurt, but we're so scared."

We shed tears and hugged each other.

I stepped inside, and my mouth dropped open. Crumbled bricks from the fireplace littered the living room. The sliding glass door leading to the patio had shattered, leaving a gaping hole. Two hutches that had been bolted to the wall lay facedown, leaving Mom's Japanese doll collection and fine china scattered everywhere. I tried to move some debris from the sofa but couldn't lift it, even with Mom's help.

Wall hangings hung askew. With broken dishes, smashed appliances and food cluttering the floor, I couldn't enter the kitchen. Even the microwave flew clear across the room.

We thanked the Lord that He had spared our lives and homes. It turned out that we were only a few miles from the epicenter of the deadly 6.7 quake in Northridge, California, about 20 miles northwest of Los Angeles.

Not everyone escaped harm. Though the 4:31 a.m. quake lasted less than 45 seconds, many died and thousands were injured. Sections of freeway crumbled. Buildings shifted off their foundations. Granada Hills Hospital collapsed and Northridge Fashion Mall suffered extensive damage.

For days, my townhome tottered with violent aftershocks, so I slept in my car in a vacant lot across the street. Others followed suit. Soon the empty lot became a city of cars with people living in them.

When I gathered enough courage, I clambered up the stairs to survey my bedroom.

A six-foot long, four-foot high bookcase-headboard made of solid, heavy wood perched on top of chopstick-thin wood extensions from my platform bed. I had always thought it didn't look safe but figured it would never move because of its weight. *Wrong!* Amazingly, the bookcase shifted but stayed precariously balanced. If it had moved a centimeter more, it would have crushed me.

With a grateful heart, I thanked God for His protection. We can never know what even the next moment may bring.

Therefore you also be ready, for the Son of Man is coming at an hour you do not expect. (Luke 12:40 NKJV)

~ Pauline Nishida
Campus Crusade for Christ

෯ ✣ ∽

High Flight

At a filmmaking conference, I rushed into an empty restaurant and pressed the MESSAGE button on my cell phone. Both of my brothers had left urgent messages. Jim said in anguish, "Dad has taken a turn for the worse, but stay in Denver until your conference is over." My other brother left a similar message.

My heart quickened. It felt like my breath had been sucked out of my lungs, and I stifled a sob. A kind waitress came over, concern on her face. "Are you all right?"

I could barely get the words out. "My daddy . . . he's not doing well . . . he . . . I just saw him a few weeks ago, and he was fine . . . but in the last few weeks . . ."

"Let me bring you some tea. Do you want some?"

"That would really be nice . . . thank you so much."

She patted my arm. "It's gonna be okay, honey."

In a stupor, I looked out the big picture window in front of my table. It was the tail end of a wild storm. *What a view.* I grabbed my cell phone and dialed my younger brother.

I could hear the anxiety in Jim's voice when he answered the phone. Jim was a retired fireman paramedic, and I could tell this was beyond tough for him. I could hear Daddy in the background laboring to breathe. It just about did me in. I wanted to be there, and I started crying. "Oh, Jim . . . I'm so sorry. I hate that you are going through this. I want to fly over and be with all of you—"

"No, stay in Denver. We have no idea how long it might be—days, weeks—only the Lord knows. But sing for Dad. I'll hold my cell phone up to his ear."

By some miracle of grace, I was able to sing the first verse of about every hymn I had ever learned, and I did it without crying. The waitress slipped me my cup of tea with an encouraging smile, and I just kept quietly singing.

"Your singing has calmed Dad," Jim said. "He even has a smile on his face."

After a few more loving words, we hung up. I stared out the picture window at the ever-deepening golden hues of the clouds at dusk. My mind flitted from one memory to another.

I reflected on what an amazing man my father is and how he had overcome much in his life. He was an orphan by the time he turned eighteen and married my mother a few years later. He worked his way up to become a brigadier general in the USAF.

Daddy and my mother never lost their childlike wonder and appreciation for their lives. Their faith in Jesus Christ as their Savior grew through the years. They had been married almost sixty-seven years when my mother passed away.

He always said to me, "Oh, Annie, I miss your mother so much. I want to go home to be with her and Jesus."

His short-term memory was bad, but he could still remember his favorite poem, "High Flight" by John Gillespie Magee Jr., written during World War II. Daddy's face glowed every time he recited the poem. I could hear his words:

Oh! I have slipped the surly bonds of Earth
And danced the skies on laughter-silvered wings;

Sunward I've climbed, and joined the tumbling mirth
of sun-split clouds, – and done a hundred things
You have not dreamed of – wheeled and soared and swung
High in the sunlit silence. Hov'ring there,
I've chased the shouting wind along and flung
My eager craft through footless halls of air . . .

Up, up the long, delirious, burning blue
I've topped the wind-swept heights with easy grace
Where never lark nor ever eagle flew –
And, while with silent lifting mind I've trod
The high untrespassed sanctity of space,
Put out my hand, and *touched the face of God*.[1]

Now, sitting in a Denver restaurant, longing to be home with Daddy, I focused on the magnificent display of clouds playing outside the picture window. I froze with disbelief at what I saw.

A perfectly defined cloud picture appeared in the shape of a gaunt, strained face of a man with his mouth open wide, as though gasping for breath. His eyes were closed in pain. A white sheet covered him up to his chest.

Then a hand from heaven reached down toward the tortured face. The vision lasted for several minutes, which was remarkable, considering the fast-changing clouds surrounding it after the storm.

A plethora of clouds swirled around in shades of magenta but with a solid cloud-picture straight from heaven! I reflected on Daddy's favorite poem and heard his words echo inside me:

Where never lark nor ever eagle flew –
And, while with silent lifting mind I've trod
The high untrespassed sanctity of space,
Put out my hand, and *touched the face of God*.[2]

I no longer cried. I no longer pined to be with my earthly father. I knew God had sent a most remarkable sign. He was with my daddy and brothers, just as He was with me in that restaurant. I was in awe of our heavenly Father.

The next morning Jim called. "Daddy went home to be with Jesus and our mother. He was thrashing and gasping for air. It was awful, but then he looked past me, over my shoulder, and stopped struggling. I looked to see who had come into the room, but no one was there. Then suddenly Daddy reached up his hand as if he took hold of an invisible hand and held on to it."

I choked back a sob. "Did he say anything?"

"I asked him if it was Jesus. And, Annie, he nodded his head."

What a comfort this has been. Daddy *slipped the surly bonds of earth* and *touched the face of God.*

I have fought the good fight, I have finished the course, I have kept the faith. (2 Timothy 4:7)

~ Ann Ault, filmmaker, actress, author and singer

1-2. "High Flight" a poem by John Gillespie Magee Jr. Public Domain.

☞ 🕊 ☜

A Divine Do-Over

I ignored the look of defeat in my husband's eyes and launched into inquisition mode. "Lined up any job interviews? Sent out any resumes?"

"There's nothing, Jen."

Bitterness soured my stomach as I sucked in a lungful of air. Steve's gotten us into this mess and was doing absolutely nothing to get us out of it. Six months earlier, he'd left a stable position as an area director for a transportation company. His sudden unemployment left us in dire financial circumstances.

Later I understood why Steve left his job. After years of long hours and being on call, he took a new job in Louisiana. His new position required even longer hours, and he had a boss that threatened and manipulated him. He quit this job to keep from spiraling deeper into depression.

"How can there be nothing?" I inhaled then exhaled slowly. "What about that sales job you told me about?"

He looked down, a frown etched across his face. "I don't want to do that."

"Whatever." I stormed out before he could see my tears brimming just below the surface.

He met me in the kitchen a moment later and grabbed me

from behind. "I need you to be strong."

Tears flooded my face as his words sank deep into my heart. Unable to respond, I turned to God in prayer. *Lord, please help us. Provide for us.*

Would we make it through this with our marriage and love still intact?

He wrapped his arms around me, and I fell against his chest, closing my eyes to the piles of boxes filling our living room. Boxes that would soon go into storage indefinitely.

"Did the Realtor call back?"

He nodded. "She'll be here to take pictures on Tuesday."

"Do you think we'll be able to sell?"

"I hope so." Steve's blue eyes glazed with moisture, and his voice cracked—the closest he'd come to crying in our eleven years of marriage. "But with the way the builders are cutting their prices, we'll have to sell at a reduced rate."

"How reduced?" No doubt we were going to lose a sizeable chunk of money—the only question was how much.

My husband enveloped the back of my head with his hand. "I don't know."

I didn't voice the question that burned in my mind: What if we didn't sell? How long would our savings sustain us with such a large mortgage—a mortgage that was manageable on my husband's previous salary but now threatened to bury us?

For two months we lived on savings. I found a job driving a bus for a local daycare center while my husband took temporary jobs. Our monthly income totaled about half of our expenditures. My anxiety mounted with each savings withdrawal, and my depression grew deeper and deeper.

One morning anger consumed me, and I could barely muster the strength to pray. Grabbing my Bible from my bedside table, I randomly flipped to Proverbs 14:1. "The wise woman builds her house, but the foolish tears it down with her own hands."

Our little girl happened into my room at just that moment, sleep still in her eyes, a stuffed rabbit clutched in her hands.

"Momma, snuggle?"

I choked back the tears and moved aside. She hopped in next to me and nestled into my arms.

Swallowing down a lump in my throat, I closed my eyes in prayer. *Lord, help me make it through this. Help me to trust You. Help me to show her what it means to trust in You.*

Two weeks later, my husband packed his bags and headed for a temporary contract job six hours away. This began the next leg of our journey. Each Monday he'd leave at four a.m., drive six hours to San Antonio and stay there until Friday, then drive home that evening.

He walked into our home, exhausted from lack of sleep and a long workweek.

I met him in the hall. "I've got good news. Sort of."

He dropped his bag on the floor and reached for me.

I allowed a partial hug, my body stiff in his arms. A moment later I pulled away and squared my shoulders. "Cathy called. We got an offer on the house." I glanced toward our daughter's bedroom, relief and anxiety swirling together in a gut-wrenching mass of emotions. "We'll lose about ten thousand," which was much better than we had expected, but it still left one glaring problem. "Where are we going to live?"

My husband sighed. "You guys could come with me to San Antonio."

"And stay in the hotel?"

"We'll figure it out."

Monday came much too quickly, and once again I was left alone with my fears. Only now, instead of running from God in anger, I turned to Him in prayer. I clung to the verse God gave me and recited it often.

Church became my lifeline. Sunday carried me to Wednesday, and Wednesday carried me to the next Sunday.

Through each message, God assured me that He'd carry us through—that He would fight for our family and our marriage.

The pastor showed a powerful podcast of a family destroyed by addiction but transformed by prayer. At the end of the service, he gave an altar call. It was as if God Himself stood at the pulpit and called each of us to come and trust Him. The entire congregation migrated down the aisles, tears streaming down countless faces.

I followed and crumpled to the floor in silent prayer. *Lord, You know what I want. I want a do-over. I want Steve to ask for his old area director job back.* As if they'd give it to him.

Less than a year previously, Steve had left them high and dry. No two weeks' notice. No explanation. Nothing but a letter of resignation sent in the mail. Now I was asking, begging God to clean up the mess.

I didn't know God was working on my husband that same night, building that same desire for his initial job.

The next morning he called me. "I've decided to contact Larry.* I'm going to ask for my old job back, if he'll take me."

"You want to go back to your old company? Seriously? But why?"

"It's the right thing. My old company keeps popping into my mind out of nowhere. And I keep getting these phone calls from my old coworkers telling me to call Larry. This has to be from God."

"Do you think Larry will let you come back?"

He sighed. "I don't know."

Yet I did. I knew God had heard me that night when I cried out in desperation. He showed up at just the right time.

Two days later, Steve returned home, and we sat at the kitchen table.

A smile tugged at his mouth. "I called Larry."

"Yeah? What'd you say?"

"I told him I'd made a mistake and wanted to come back.

If he'd take me."

I swallowed, anxiety nibbling at my gut. "What'd he say?"

"It's not for sure, but he's going to make a few calls, see if he can get it approved. I think I've got a shot. Larry made it sound like he'd give me a temporary position until a director's position opens up."

I grabbed his hands and gave a squeeze. "Oh, Steve, that's wonderful."

Steve returned to his old company but under a new boss. He returned stronger, equipped with boundaries and a resolve to maintain the balance necessary for his health and our marriage.

It's been five years since God restored all that we lost and more. We have a home of our own, two cars, and steady employment.

Yet I wouldn't trade a day of our past for anything, because in that moment of total brokenness, God showed me His tender mercy. He reminded me that He does indeed hear us when we call. He showed me that no situation is beyond His redeeming power. No mistake is beyond His repair.

And my God shall supply all your need according to His riches in glory by Christ Jesus. (Philippians 4:19 NKJV)

~ Jennifer Slattery, freelance writer
jenniferslatterylivesoutloud.com

* Names have been changed to protect privacy.

Mundaka Ride

Massive, pitching and heaving set waves up to twelve feet lifted me up on my surfboard. With every ounce of strength, I paddled my weary arms in frenzied bouts and swerved my board forward. I was about to get a wave in when someone farther up the line jumped in and yelled, "Got it!"

"Ugh, not again!" The large surf weighed on my mind as my strength ebbed away with the outgoing tide. I'd been in the water for over five hours and was not only completely spent, but also in dire need of food and water since I hadn't eaten or drunk anything all day, adding to my extreme exhaustion.

"Lord, I'm about to get caught inside one of the huge set waves breaking right on top of me." I let out a heavy pant. "If I don't get a wave in soon, I could receive a severe pounding into the sandbar or break my neck like the Australian pro surfer did this morning. Please help me to catch a wave that will carry me in for that last ride, since I'm too exhausted to paddle in."

Earlier that day, surfers from around the world poured into the small, picturesque town of Mundaka in Northern Spain where my family and I were taking a respite.

We'd arrived a few days before a powerful storm battered the North Atlantic. I found myself at the right place and right time to score some of the best cylindrical waves at Europe's famed point break known as Mundaka.

Straddling my board, my thoughts flitted. *Will I make my speaking engagement in France this evening?* It certainly wouldn't bode well for future invitations if I missed it.

Ever since I received the baptism of the Holy Spirit, my faith stabilized and my life changed dramatically. I left my past career in fashion modeling and professional surfing to serve God full-time. He had been sending me to places all over the world to bring messages of hope and impart the gift of the Holy Spirit to people. At the same time, I'd been given these great opportunities to surf at all these wonderful places.

Once in the lineup, I heaved deep sighs. "And, Lord, help me to make my speaking engagement in time. I dread the public transportation back to France—schlepping bags and a surfboard on two buses, a subway, and two trains—a process that takes seven hours and only half the time by car."

At my most exhausted point, while continuing to push against the strong currents, something unusual happened as another wave reared up. A guy dropping in called out, "Come on, drop in, we'll ride it together."

I couldn't believe my ears. *He's actually inviting me to ride the wave with him?* This hasn't happened to me in all my years of surfing. I joined him.

The powerful wave pushed us down the line as we twisted and turned around each other. We glided down the line at rapid speeds for hundreds of yards.

The thundering roar of the crashing lip grew softer as the wave drew near its end. I stood on my board enjoying its last few moments. "Oh, Lord, thank You for this wave and all the other ones today. This happens to be the best one."

As the wave fizzled into the river mouth, I kicked out and yelled, "What an incredible wave!"

We high-fived each other and headed in different

directions. I paddled down to the long easier path through the river mouth while he headed up the direct way over the rocks.

As I staggered into our hotel lobby, my new surfer buddy happened to be talking to my wife. "Hey, we meet again." We shook hands. "I'm Bryan from California."

"Niv from Israel."

"Thanks again for that awesome wave!" After chatting a while, I looked at the clock. "Hey, this has been fun but we need to get going to Bayonne, France."

"We go there too! Why you don't ride with us?"

"I appreciate the gesture, but we have a lot of stuff and a child with us."

He glanced at his car, the size of a Geo Metro, with six surfboards on the roof and lots of luggage inside. Then his eyes traveled to his two friends. "Yeah, we get you in."

"Well, I think you're crazy, but if you want to give it a try, we'd be stoked."

He and his two friends immediately went to work packing and repacking for the next hour.

They somehow fit seven surfboards and a stroller on the roof. All of the luggage crammed into the trunk like a trash compactor. We squeezed two backpacks between our legs and sat hip-to-hip with our knees to our chests. But I didn't care, since we would reach our destination in about three hours.

Riding through the rugged coastal region, I prayed. "Thank You, Lord, for the two amazing rides today. I get the best wave of the day and a ride to France!"

"For your Father knows the things you have need of before you ask Him." (Matthew 6:8 NKJV)

~ Bryan Marleaux
www.GraceWorldMission.org

Finding Hope

My brother's baseball coach flashed a bright smile at me. "Cindy, I have a surprise for you. You're very special and pretty." His words sent an electrical current down my spine. He sent the team away for pizza and took me to his car.

As a fifteen year old, I drank in the attention he gave me. Before I knew it, he drove down a dark and deserted dirt road. He cut the engine and raped me. Then he shoved me away.

"Now, you can't say anything to anyone," he said with a smirk, "or you'll look stupid. And who would believe a grown man would take an interest in a scrawny girl like you?"

My self-esteem shattered like a broken dish, and I built a wall around me for years. If someone told me I was pretty, I'd scream, *Liar!* in my head.

Three years later that wall began to crumble. I met a young man I'll call Ruben. No matter how many times I pushed him away, he never gave up on me. "Trust me," he'd say.

Is he for real? Can I trust him? He makes me feel safe.

I fell for Ruben and became pregnant at nineteen.

Dad threw me out of the house, so I lived with my aunt.

During my pregnancy, Mom visited me and scolded me repeatedly. "How could you be so stupid? You can't trust men.

They'll cheat on you or leave you. They always do."

During my fifth month of pregnancy, my friend brought me some alarming news. "Ruben has another girl who's also pregnant—someone you know."

"I don't believe you."

Then one day I saw the girl at the mall. She shot me a scornful expression and flaunted the diamond ring on her finger. It was like someone carved my heart out with a scalpel.

That evening while I was peeling potatoes at a friend's home, some people walked in. Someone snuck up from behind me and touched my arm. "Cindy, I need to explain—"

The moment Ruben touched me, blinding rage flared inside me. The betrayal was so overwhelming that I swung the knife at him and slashed him. I didn't flinch. He grabbed a towel from the kitchen counter and held it to his body.

Gritting my teeth, I screamed, "Get out!"

That night I sat in the shower and wailed. *Never again will I let anyone get close to me.*

After my daughter was born, she stole my dad's heart. Mom took care of my daughter on weekends, and I spent time with my friends—drinking, getting high, and selling drugs.

I could only let a man touch me when I was loaded—numb and unfeeling. I met a physically abusive drug dealer, and it wasn't long before I became pregnant again. I couldn't tell my parents. I took all kinds of drugs, hoping it would cause a miscarriage. Nothing worked. Finally I went to a clinic to have an abortion. After three schedule changes, they told me I couldn't abort the baby because I was too far along. I gave birth to another girl and caught my parents' wrath again.

Several years later, two men abducted and raped me. They beat me and nearly killed me. I couldn't function after that. *My kids would be better off without me.* I overdosed on pills.

Instead of dying, I awoke in a psychiatric ward and wove in and out of consciousness. The doctor said to my dad, "The medication she took has affected her heart. She may not last through the night. If you have a priest, call him."

In a rasping voice, I begged Dad, "Take care of my girls."

Three months later, I was released and went back to my aunt's home. I hid my pain with drugs and alcohol.

Why do horrible things keep happening to me? Was it the way I looked or dressed? I never wanted to be noticed again, so I ate and ate to gain weight. Men won't want a fat girl.

My life became a destructive whirlwind, and we partied at the house weekly, Thursday through Monday. During this time, my two cousins attended a women's ministry at Jubilee Christian Center. My daughter wanted to go but was too young to drive. So I took her and waited for her in the main sanctuary.

"Mom, I enjoy church and want to go back again."

"I'll take you as long as you don't talk to me about God, and we're home in time for my parties. Got it?" She nodded.

I'd take Olga to church with two lines of crank up my nostrils and three shots of tequila.

One day, the pastor prayed for my daughter and she fell.

What are you doing? Get off the floor!

On the way home, I yelled at her. "Don't ever embarrass me like that again, or I'll never bring you to church again!"

"But, Mom, I didn't fall on purpose. I felt the power of God go through me."

A month later, Olga went up for prayer again and looked at me funny. I mouthed, "I'm going outside for a smoke." Then a powerful emotion engulfed me, and I started crying.

What's happening to me? I tried to pull myself together.

A woman approached me. "Do you want prayer?"

"Will it stop me from crying?"

She looked at me puzzled. "Are you saved?"

"What does that mean?"

"Would you like to say the sinner's prayer with me?"

"If it'll make me stop crying."

The minute I received Christ into my life, the high from the crank was gone, the buzz from alcohol left and the desire for the cigarette I held in my hand vanished. It was like someone gave me a blood transfusion and hot shower, sanitizing my entire body inside and out.

I went home, and my friends were waiting for us on the deck with drugs and alcohol. I squeezed past them all, and announced, "We're not doing this here anymore."

Puzzled faces stared at me. "What happened to you?"

"I received Christ."

They looked at me as if I'd found a new drug.

Later that night Olga said, "Mom, my prayer request was for you to experience the power of God."

"He certainly came on me before I could leave the room."

I understand why I couldn't abort this child. Olga is a very special gift from God.

Every week for six months, my old friends called me to see if they could come over and party. My answer was still no. I *never* went back.

Although I no longer drank or did drugs, I had to deal with my hurts, anger, and other habits. Pastor Ida worked with me on a weekly basis for a year and a half. A whole new life began to unfold for me as I spent time praying and studying the Bible.

Later I joined Celebrate Recovery, a nationwide program that helps people overcome their addictions with God's help.

Today, I am one of the life coaches in the program. It's my passion to help people become all that God created them to be. No matter what happened in the past, there's always hope.

God is our merciful Father and the source of all comfort.
(2 Corinthians 1:3 NLT)

~ Cindy Nanez

Somersault

My husband pulled our sedan onto the cracked driveway of a faded white Colonial. At one time this derelict structure had no doubt boasted Southern charm. Now its grimy windows, broken shutters, and courtyard landscaped with dirt, weeds, and discarded bottles gave testament of its losing battles with subtropical weather and neglect.

I let out a sardonic laugh at my husband's sense of humor. "Thomas, this is not funny. Take us to where we're going to be living. The kids and I are tired."

He turned to me with the most serious facial expression I've ever seen. "Dwan, I'm not joking. It's the only house on New Orleans's West Bank that fits our budget and is big enough for our furniture. The others were just too small or expensive."

This rundown, battered house was to be our home?

Our six-year-old daughter, Serrae, yelled from the backseat, "Daddy, I'm scared. It looks like a haunted house."

Four-year-old Noah chimed in. "Does it have a backyard?"

Thomas pressed his hand to his forehead. "Listen, it's not as bad as it looks. It's not haunted. The house just needs some cleaning up. The backyard is huge. It has an Olympic-size pool, six bedrooms, plenty of room for all your stuff. This is temporary until my job transfers me back to Houston."

He turned to the children. "One more thing. Kids, stay close to me and Mommy until we get the house ready."

I shot my husband a look. How were we going to transform a fifty-year-old disaster area into a home?

He opened the front door, and I gagged at the damp odor that swept over me. I could almost taste the stale, musty stench.

I stepped over the threshold, and my eyes were drawn to a steep, narrow staircase—every mother's nightmare.

"Thomas, that looks dangerous. See how the wood is uneven in spots? It's probably slippery too. We'll have to watch the kids as they go up and down."

After surveying the muddied Berber carpet with runs in the seams and the tiny kitchen with missing cabinets and cockroach baits scattered about, hopelessness set in. "Thomas, I don't think I can stay here. I've never lived like this before."

He wrapped his arms around me tightly. "God is with us wherever we are. Everything will be okay. Anywhere the Father takes us is home."

After pest fumigation, carpet steam cleaning—twice—and a month of continual disinfecting, the grime abated, and the tumbledown two-story was livable.

The children, although frightened to sleep in their own beds, enjoyed the plethora of rooms during the day. Constantly aware of the dangers of the ramshackle Colonial, I was careful to keep an eye on the kids as they bounced between rooms.

One day my son and I were walking downstairs. He let go of the handrail, dashed in front, and ran toward the bottom.

My warning, "Wait, Noah!" was not even out of my mouth.

He bounced into the air and started to descend headfirst toward the bottom step. I cried out, "Lord, help! Suddenly, all my fears of this place haunted me. *He's going to die.*

As I watched this scene unfold, I was powerless to stop the

impending tragedy. Noah was too far ahead of me to cushion his fall. But just then, the most amazing thing happened.

Noah, who had never demonstrated any athletic, much less gymnastic skills, stretched his hand out.

Instead of landing on his head, his hand hit the steps, breaking his fall. The remarkable spectacle before my eyes didn't stop there. Rather than his little arm collapsing under the weight of his body, he pushed off the step, over into a perfect somersault. He then cascaded over the last two steps and landed feetfirst on the hardwood entry below.

He stood at the base of the steps with his arms held high, smiling at me like an Olympian who just won the gold medal.

I rushed to the bottom of the stairs, grabbed Noah, and held him in my shaking arms. "Noah, are you okay? You scared me! How did you learn to do a flip?"

He looked at me with a surprised yet questioning expression. "I don't know, Mommy. I just touched the steps and flipped over."

I thanked God for doing what I couldn't do—even with my watchful mother eyes—protecting my son from a dangerous fall. As I lay in bed that night, I pondered what could have happened, but also what God had done. The Father cushions us from many stumbles in life, and He gives us the strength to endure.

My husband's words on the day of our arrival rang in my ears: "God is with us wherever we are. Everything will be okay. Anywhere He takes us is home."

For He will give His angels charge concerning you, to guard you in all your ways. (Psalm 91:11)

~ Dwan Reed, freelance writer and speaker
dwanreed.com

❧ 🕊 ☙

Make a Difference

Heart racing, I took a second look at my neighbor as she forced her German shepherd to pull her wheelchair and obese body down the condo hallway.

She yanked her dog's leash. "Move it, stupid!" *Swat.* You could barely hear his yelp.

This was Toronto, different from my small hometown where everybody got involved in everyone's business, so I doubted anyone would report her. Rushing to escape to the elevator, I wondered if I was any better.

She spotted me and called in her thick, gravelly voice. "Cheryl . . . Come here."

"Oh, hi, Racelle. I'm just on my way to class."

Her eyes became desperate; her jack-o-lantern grin, pitiful. "I need you to stop by later this afternoon. I wanna spend some time with ya."

I'd been in her condo half a dozen times, and the reality was I'd rather sit on nails then spend my prime time between work and school squirming on her itchy, dirty dog-haired sofa.

Invite her to church.

Where did that thought come from? Was that Jesus?

Healing evangelist Billy Burke was coming to town next

week. Did God want me to take her? If I didn't ask now, I'd chicken out. "Racelle, would you like to come to a special healing meeting with me?"

"A Christian meeting?"

"Ah . . . yeah."

She shook her head, cackling a laugh. "I'm Jewish!"

"Jesus was Jewish. Besides, you've got nothing to lose. It'll be a neat experience."

She blew air from her pursed lips. "Dear, dear, Cheryl. You know I don't believe in all that crap, but, okay, I will come to your healing thing."

"You will?" I let the words sink in. "Great. I'll look forward to it!"

Whenever someone knocked on my door that week, I thought it was Racelle coming to cancel. No such knock. I went from elation to worry. What if she made a scene? What if she got mad and cussed at the man? What if people thought she was my mother!

After a week, the night finally came. Racelle dressed in her usual, worn-out clothes. Wheel-Trans dropped us off at the front entrance, and I wondered if I'd see anybody I knew. The instant the door opened, we were greeted by bright lights and loud, celebrative music. People's faces shone with anticipation. Mine had sweat.

When the worship began, Racelle wiped a strand of matted hair from her eyes and belted out the songs as if she knew them. I glanced left and right, upping my volume.

Billy, a gentleman in his late thirties, stepped onto the platform in a suit as white as his smile. God-praises flowed from his lips. "How many of you know that we're all God's instruments? God is the healer. Not me."

The room quieted as he talked about how the same Jesus who healed people in the New Testament had healed him of brain cancer when he was a child. "God never changes. The

One who laid down His life to forgive sins still heals people today."

Billy scanned the crowd. "Does anyone want healing?"

Racelle shouted, "I do!" She tugged on my sleeve. "Let's get up there. Excuse me, excuse me." Racelle snaked her wheelchair in and out of a crowd with such speed and carelessness that I wondered if anyone would need healing from bruises.

A long line formed in front of the platform. Billy didn't take long to get to us, thank God. Racelle had already stepped out of her wheelchair on trembling legs and was squeezing me and the wheelchair.

"What's the trouble?" he asked.

"I have muscular dystrophy."

"What's your name?"

"Racelle."

Billy placed his hand on her head and prayed with passion. "Father God, please touch Racelle's body. Muscular dystrophy, I *command* you to *Go!* In Jesus' name."

Racelle jolted as if hit by electricity. She collapsed backward, but someone caught her and laid her gently down.

"Stand up again," he said, extending his hand.

"I can't. It feels like something zapped me."

He chuckled. "God just touched your body."

She grabbed his hand and did what he asked. With one leg in front of the other, she stepped forward. She then took several well-balanced steps.

"Keep going," he said. "You can do it." And she did. "Praise God! Jesus is healing you. Say, 'Thank You, Jesus.'"

The words shook through her with laughter. "Thank You, Jesus." She said it again, only louder. She picked up her pace, turning her walk into a run. Her stiff arms clawed the air in rapid motion with her legs. She raced around the room while everyone broke into claps and cheers.

I was stunned. I'd known this lady for two years. She could barely stand. Tonight she was running and giving thanks to Jesus, whom just minutes before she didn't believe in.

Tears coursed down her face like a cleansing stream, streaking away dirt in their lines. A sob escaped my throat.

I thought about how Satan might try deception to draw her away from God, who loved her and healed her. We'd just experienced a small glimpse of heaven, and I refused to let fear darken it.

"Who healed you?" Billy asked.

"Jesus."

"Do you believe in Him?"

"Yes."

Billy looked at me. "Did you bring her?" I nodded.

He turned to an older gentleman. "Can I borrow your hat?" The gentleman handed it to him. Billy looked at me and said, "We're going to take up an offering so you can buy this lady some clothes. Sound good?"

I nodded, glancing at Racelle as she beamed. This was surely a new kind of love for her.

Later that evening Racelle pushed her wheelchair as we slipped into the crisp night air. She looked taller than I remembered. As she entered her condo, I giggled. Even her dog would be surprised. Clearly, the rays of God's mercy stretched farther than eyes could see.

Jesus healed an unbelieving woman who hadn't walked in years. At the same time, he touched the limping faith of a simple college girl, giving her a story she'd run with for years.

He sent His word and healed them. (Psalm 107:20 NKJV)

~ Cheryl Ricker, author of *A Friend in the Storm*

A Calm after the Storm

Grief cut like a jagged piece of broken glass, and I found it hard to breathe. I had just hit my fourth month of pregnancy and sat in the doctor's office shell-shocked. All I heard was "the baby has cysts on his brain . . . possible Down syndrome." The doctor's voice droned on as he explained the ultrasound results.

Usually I cry when I'm upset. Instead of my emotions boiling to the surface, they sucked me under, down deep into a place of fear and confusion. I recalled the day I discovered I was pregnant. It surprised and delighted our whole family. We already had five children, but my husband, Scott, and I were thrilled to add this little miracle to our brood. Now, at thirty-nine years old, it was like the Lord struck me with tragedy.

"I don't think we'll do any further testing," I said to the doctor. "We're Christians and don't believe in abortion."

That night the tidal wave of tears hit, and I sat in my prayer chair and wept aloud. "Why are you doing this, Lord? You made the heavens and the earth. It's easy for You to knit us a healthy baby."

After recovering from the shock, I called my prayer partners and church prayer hotline. Soon people from our congregation somberly approached me, concern and love on their faces. "We are praying for your baby. May the Lord heal your child." Many quoted Scripture verses. "Trust in the Lord with all your heart and believe in God's promises" was the theme that arose as the dark days dragged on.

Scott said little, but his calm, steady strength comforted me. "We need to surrender this. This baby comes from the Lord. He is the child God has chosen for us to raise."

I'd read that many Down syndrome babies died in the womb. If they lived, they often needed medical attention for the rest of their lives.

Our woefully inadequate medical insurance didn't cover much. We already struggled financially, raising our other children. I cried nearly every day, but one predawn morning while sitting by a warm fire, I accepted God's will. An overwhelming peace flooded my spirit.

Soon after that, Scott and I told our pastor about the ultrasound results. The pastor prayed, "Thank You, God, for the baby in Paula's womb. We praise You for the gift of life." Then his prayer took on a confident, eager air. "We believe You, Lord, that this baby will be born healthy. We are trusting You for this. Yes, we believe and trust You," he repeated in a strikingly sure voice.

Faith flowed into me. The type of faith in which I believed God for a healthy baby.

Yet, sometimes I awoke in the middle of the night with cold air upon me. Would our baby die? If our son lived, would I spend the rest of my life caring for this child? Lifelong dreams of pursuing a career vanished.

Looking out the window at the bright stars with tears soaking my pillow, I whispered, "I love You, Lord. You hold the universe in Your hands. Our baby belongs to You. Whether You give us a sick or healthy baby, I choose to be grateful. After all, children are a blessing from You, Lord."

Promises from the Bible burned through my heart and mind. Scriptures about children gave me hope and began to outweigh my anxious thoughts.

Christmas came and went, along with my fortieth birthday. With my big belly, I found it difficult to lean close to the table and inhale deeply to blow out all the candles.

I went into labor in January and gave birth to Baby Garry. The next day the doctor admitted my newborn to the Neonatal Intensive Care unit due to a heart complication. A battery of tests followed.

When the cardiologist approached us, we asked, "So our son has Down syndrome?"

The young cardiologist snapped, "Who told you that?"

"The ultrasound showed our baby had cysts on his brain," I said teary-eyed, "that Down syndrome could cause—"

"There are no cysts, and your baby does not have Down syndrome. We think he aspirated [swallowed] the fluid during birth, which may be temporarily affecting his heart. We are going to keep an eye on him, but it should clear up just fine."

Relief like an overflowing waterfall flooded me.

Follow-up exams showed that our baby's heart healed perfectly. Had things gone the other way, God would still have gotten the glory since Down children are special and unite families and communities together.

My grateful spirit soared heavenward.

Today our three-year-old son, Garry, is an energetic, healthy, blond toddler who says his prayers every night in his bunk bed with his brothers.

Do not fear, for I am with you; do not anxiously look about you, for I am your God. (Isaiah 41:10)

~ Paula Bicknell

꙰ 🕊 ꙰

Mob Connection

The lure of the underworld possessed me. During the day I worked as a police officer. At night I visited the Mob dives and pushed drugs through "The Pizza Connection," which were some pizzerias across America that served as fronts for narcotics. I mixed drugs and alcohol and craved more of the Mob lifestyle—money and everything it could buy.

My Mob connection came from my great-grandfather, a famous *don* and chief of police in Calabria, Italy. He didn't care how he acquired money, power, and prestige. He had joined forces with the Black Hand—a secret society that later became the Calabrese Mafia. The Calabrese and Sicilian Mafias came to the U.S. and merged to form the Mob as we know it today.

I got married and had a beautiful baby girl, Racquel. In the Mob tradition, I kept a mistress on the side, but all these things didn't satisfy me. I looked for something to fill the emptiness.

One day, Tony came over and handed me a stash of coke. "Hold this package for me."

The following day, he returned with another man.

"Rocco, I need that package back," Tony said. "I want to introduce you to another friend I do business with, who's going to move a large quantity of coke for us."

Tony took the drugs from me and handed me money.

Why is he giving me money? It's a setup. The man with Tony turned out to be an undercover agent.

Shock, betrayal, and anger raged through me like a burning inferno. The S.W.A.T. team invaded my house. I tossed aside a concealed gun I had on me, fearing they would kill me if they found me armed. I raised my arms. "Look, I have nothing on me."

After they took me to jail, five detectives gathered around me in the interrogation room. One red-haired undercover agent set his mug down and leaned in. "If you give us the boss, we'll work a deal with the DA for no time in prison."

"Be a wise guy informant? I'm not a snitch like Tony. I want to stay alive. Not be a walking dead man!"

For six weeks, I had them on a merry-go-round, feeding them bits of useless information. The Mob put out a contract on the guy who squealed. Who betrayed me? Tony, my "best friend!" Who was to fulfill that contract? Me!

While out on bail, I went to my doctor friend, Frank Iozzi. For years he patched me up and talked about Jesus, but I only half listened. This "Christian stuff" wasn't for me. Besides, I was *the* ROCCO MORELLI and could take care of myself.

"Rocco, I have some extra tickets for a Full Gospel Business Men's dinner," Frank said. "Why don't you come hear the man who worked as a teamster for Jimmy Hoffa. I know you'll enjoy him. You and your guests can join me for a delicious sit-down dinner at the Holiday Inn."

I shrugged, but figured I had nothing to lose. "Okay."

The boys in the Mafia say, "Keep your enemies closer than a friend." I decided to take Tony. What a perfect alibi.

In the hotel banquet room, I saw people smiling and hugging one another. *Did they all win the lottery?*

We sat down—my "best friend" beside me. Then everyone stood, sang and declared, "Praise the Lord!"

What a bunch of characters.

Tony looked uncomfortable, but not me.

I planned to carry out the contract and do away with my former buddy after dinner to get revenge and Mob status. But after the speaker Steve Totin started, I got so caught up in his speech, I forgot Tony was even there. I could relate to Steve.

Tony left, but something kept me glued to my seat. *Could Jesus really change my life? Can He really fill the empty spot in me?* It seemed like Steve was talking directly to me. When the prayer line formed, I joined the others. Here I was about to do away with Tony and go to prison for numerous Mob crimes, and I waited in a prayer line, as if an unseen magnet drew me.

When my turn came, I found myself asking Jesus to forgive me and come into my heart as Steve directed.

Jesus came. Rocco Morelli, tough mobster, never felt more humble. A peace and joy I'd never experienced before came over me. The power-hungry Mafia craving that had plagued me all these years vanished, and I left that place as a new man.

Even though I began a new life with Christ, I had to pay a price for my past crimes. The Scripture says, "What you sow, you also reap." My sentence could have been twenty years, but the judge reduced it to two.

In prison, I studied the Bible daily. I talked to many inmates about God, and they listened to me because I used to be one of them. Even the most hard-core criminals softened when I told them, "Jesus loves you."

Steve Totin invited me to give my testimony on Cornerstone Television. I was the first inmate to appear on his show. Collect phone calls began to pour in from prisoners across the country. CTV attended to their needs and paid for all expenses. The prison ministry was born.

Prison garb and jail bars became such a large part of my existence that I could scarcely believe it when the parole board released me. Mom and Dad took me home and welcomed me.

"Mom, you must have prayed really hard. I can't believe the judge reduced my sentence to fifteen months."

"Rocco, I prayed for you daily that God would have mercy on you and put a hedge of protection around you."

The next few years I struggled as an entrepreneur with a criminal record. The Holy Spirit never let me fall back into my old lifestyle. I began a career with a Fortune 500 company and became a divisional sales distributor.

I continued my business career and started my own ministry while pursuing my education. I later completed my degree in theology and became an ordained pastor.

Life wasn't easy. I made mistakes—not Mafia type but some. I divorced twice, yet I yearned for a loving spouse.

A striking young blonde caught my attention at a Full Gospel Business Men's dinner I spoke at. I sensed the Holy Spirit nudging me and assuring me that she was "the one." During the months that ensued, Christine and I bonded, and we pledged our wedding vows.

We owned and operated several businesses until the Lord directed us to sell everything and move to Florida. We launched our ministries for the lost, hurting, at-risk youth, victims of crime, prisoners, and their families.

I'm grateful my mom never stopped praying for me, and God kept His hand on me, sending His angels to protect me.

Today when I'm back at prison, it's not as an inmate but to share God's message of hope with them.

Therefore, if anyone is in Christ, he is a new creation; the old has gone, the new has come! (2 Corinthians 5:17 NIV)

~ Rocco Morelli
www.roccomorelli.org

෧ 🕊 ෨

Angel in Flip-Flops

Iridescent strokes of red and orange splashed across the horizon as the sun slipped below the distant ridge. I drank in the sight of the mountainous hills that cascaded in gradual waves to the water's edge.

My husband, David, and I lived in the beautiful Okanagan valley, a destination spot in B.C. Canada, but rarely took the time to appreciate it. This weekend's respite was long overdue.

Familiarity gave way to new territory as we meandered down a windy stretch of road. Dusk fought valiantly to push the edges of daylight into submission as the sky steadily darkened.

"Blossom, we better find this place soon, or we'll never have enough light to set up. Keep your eyes peeled." A hint of worry laced his words. "I clocked the miles, and we should find a dirt road that heads down to the lake anytime now."

The miles continued to roll by. His shoulders tensed, and he fidgeted uneasily in his seat.

"That must be it," we shouted together, spotting the gravel lane.

"It looks a little bumpy," he said. "I guess since this place is seasonal, they don't worry about it much."

Bumpy became rough. Rough turned into jagged terrain. A severe grinding noise made me wince. A nasty rock hit the bottom of our GMC cargo van.

"You've got to be kidding," he huffed and slammed his fist on the dashboard. "This can't be the right road." Frustration mounted; his knuckles whitened on the steering wheel. "First chance I get, we're turning around."

It was too late. A vertical bank hugged us on one side, and a steep cliff dropped off on the other. The narrow passageway forward was our only option. No way could our two-wheel drive, bucket of bolts back up the hill we just descended.

David's face blanched. We inched forward.

I began to pray silently, pleading for safety.

The van groaned. It lurched and scraped over another large boulder. A deep rut cut across the road and caught us in its evil grip. The wheels spun wildly, spitting up a cloud of dust as thick as coastal fog. Back and forth the van rocked as we tried to escape. The hole only deepened.

A trickle of sweat ran down my spine, and dread fell upon me as the severity of the situation hit me. We were miles from civilization and darkness loomed ominously. I was pregnant and exhausted. Dusk had done little to decrease the muggy heat, and our dog thought it was time to disembark and play. Worst of it, David resembled Old Faithful ready to blow.

Prayer as natural as breathing flowed from my heart. I bent my head and whispered, "Dear God, help us. We have no way of getting out of here without you."

David erupted in anger. "God?" he yelled. "Tell me where God is now! It's too late for prayer."

"You handle it your way, and I'll handle it mine." I retorted with a hint of defensiveness. One look at his face told me it was not the time to battle a point.

I knew his outburst was indicative of the struggle he had with a loving God due to damage done by his earthly father.

Slamming out of the vehicle, he continued to scream to the heavens. A mixture of colorful language and desperation pierced the tranquility of the wilderness around us.

I followed to assess the situation. My mouth dropped open. We weren't slightly stuck where we could push our old jalopy out. No, we were undeniably trapped in the jaws of a monster hole. "Oh my . . ." the words petered into thin air. I could see why my husband was distressed. I stood in abject silence and again began to pray.

What happened next was nothing short of divine intervention.

"Hey. Thought I heard someone in trouble."

Startled at the sound of a voice, we turned around. A man wearing a goofy hat, cut-offs, and flip-flops approached from the opposite direction.

"Looks like you could use a little help." His eyebrows rose as he whistled between his teeth. "Wow, you're sure stuck. Don't worry. We'll have you out in a jiffy."

What? Does he think he's Superman?

David and I looked at each other in disbelief.

The stranger kept up incessant chatter while circling the vehicle in a thorough assessment. "I was out on the lake in my boat, and I heard the yelling. Call me crazy, but I just had to check it out." He laughed at his own humor.

I knew exactly what he meant. Not too many people would approach the ranting he must have heard from David.

"Took a bit to get my boat anchored, but here I am." A smile tugged at both corners of his mouth, as if he knew something we did not.

"How?" David asked.

"There just happens to be a bulldozer parked down by the beach with the key in it. Odd place for one in the middle of nowhere," he said, scratching his head. "But it'll come in mighty handy. Good thing I know how to run one of those babies. Now, don't go anywhere." He chuckled at the impossibility. "I'll be right back."

We both stood in a complete daze as we heard the rumble of a heavy machine coming our way. Then we watched this man with the expertise of a pro hook up the van to the bulldozer and pull it to the main part of the road. With a wave and a winsome smile, the mysterious stranger and bulldozer disappeared into the darkness. It wasn't until later that we realized we did not ask his name or even properly thank him.

The silence of that moment was surreal. Words penned upon this paper are inadequate. You could say it was sacred, a moment of sweet wonder. There is no question in my mind that God heard my prayer and showed up to help as any loving Father would.

All anger, fear, and anxiety melted, and in its place a reverence, awe, and thankfulness flooded in.

Reflecting back, it amazes me that on a stretch of deserted backcountry road, at twilight, on a lake eighty miles long, a guy just happens by in his boat. He hears the ranting of an angry man and cares enough to investigate. Strangely, a bulldozer is on hand with a key, and he knows how to use it. Voilà. We're on our way.

We never did get that weekend at the lake, but what we received was much more profound. God reached down and answered an immediate need in a way that could not be denied.

"Call upon Me in the day of trouble; I shall rescue you, and you will honor Me." (Psalm 50:15)

~ Blossom Turner
www.blossomturner.com

A Mirror of My Father

We stood in front of a large bathroom mirror with foamy white beards of Noxzema shaving cream covering the stubble and peach fuzz, respectively, on our faces. Dad worked his gray metal hand-held shaver up and down his face. I copied him stroke for stroke with my razor-less one, until our fresh, smooth skin was completely exposed. Holding hot hand towels to our flesh, we wiped ourselves clean, refreshed and ready to face a new day.

Dad not only showed me how to shave, but he taught me how to catch a baseball, tie a necktie, and drive a car. He also gave me my first Bible and showed self-sacrificing love to me, my family, and people in need. He introduced me to God, our Father, and Jesus, His Son.

Being a man of prayer and a few words, his words carried a lot of weight whenever he spoke. Two years before his death, I asked him, "What advice would you want to leave with your children?"

He gave me just three words. "Pray to Jesus."

Those three powerful words came alive on the day a blood clot traveled from Dad's heart to his brain and put him into a coma. I was living in New York, too far away from Gardena,

California, to be of much help. But my friends and I prayed.

On the eighth day of his coma, Dad contracted pneumonia and could hardly breathe. The doctors thought he might not last the night. They gave us the choice of either keeping him on a respirator or giving him morphine and letting him go.

This happened one day before Dad's birthday. Normally his birthdays were happy occasions, but sadness, distress, and uncertainty filled this one.

Dad had battled diseases and physical problems, including tuberculosis that put him in a special relocation camp in Canada called New Denver during World War II. It took him three years to beat.

He also underwent surgery for colon cancer, and his weak heart required a pacemaker. If God was going to take him home, I was okay with it.

In this darkest of hours, God encouraged me in an unexpected way. While shuffling through my files, I found an old folder of letters from my dad. The words in one letter jumped out at me: *We must pray for Rev. Haruyama's miraculous healing. If God wills, he will be healed.*

Justin Haruyama, my pastor at the time, was dying of liver cancer. If my dad could encourage me to pray for someone dying from an incurable disease, I certainly could pray for my father, who was "only" in a coma. He gave me the hope I needed to keep praying for him.

And Jesus kept my father alive so I could see him.

I flew home and immediately went to the ICU. I found him lying flat, eyes closed, with many tubes attached to his face and body and a respirator keeping him breathing. The doctor said, "Talk to your father in his native language."

Walking over to his side, I put my hand in his, and said in Japanese, "Dad, it's Cyril. I came from New York."

I could feel the strong grip of his hand as I told him I had been praying for him. I thanked him for the letter that encouraged me to keep praying for him. He squeezed my hand off and on, so I was certain he heard me.

I knew Jesus brought me to his side for what I did next.

Placing my other hand on his head, I prayed. "Jesus, heal Dad of any damage to his brain, any pneumonia or disease, and make him conscious."

Nothing changed, only his strong grip, but I knew I had done what the Lord sent me to do. I just stood there holding his hand, feeling him intermittently squeeze mine.

"*Aishite'ru yo* [I love you]. *Wakatte'ru, wakatte'ru* [I understand what you're trying to say]," I said.

Before I left, I had one more thing to do. When Jesus healed people, He often gave commands such as "Stretch out your hand" or "Take up your pallet and walk."

Oh, no. I can't do that with people around. But following the Lord's lead and being alone, I said in a loud voice, "Wake up!" Well, he didn't open his eyes or sit up or do anything. He just kept squeezing my hand.

But that afternoon, for the first time in eleven days, my dad responded to his doctor. He squeezed the doctor's hand on command and fluttered his eyelids when asked to open his eyes. The Lord had brought him out of the coma. The doctor called it a "small miracle."

For a few days, my father's vital signs were strong, and his white blood cell count improved. He nodded or shook his head in answer to questions. I sang his favorite hymns to him, including "Jesus Loves Me," which moved him so that even his tightly shut eyes produced a tear.

God gave me and my family time to tell Dad things we could only tell him privately. After three days, the Lord took him home.

Although I was deeply saddened, I knew the Lord had answered the prayer I had been praying all along—that He would bring my dad out of his coma so that my family and I could say good-bye to him. And He did. And we did say good-bye—for now.

As he did with his shaver, without saying a word my dad taught me something valuable—how the Lord's love and power can enter the world when we pray. So, just as the Son of God did only what He learned from his Father, I'm doing what I've learned from my dad—I'm praying to Jesus, for long periods daily. And I—and the world around me—will never be the same.

With quiet strength, you held me
With enduring wisdom, you counseled me
With wordless eloquence, you preached to me
Life's Truth by example.
Father and Son mirrored by father and son.

Honor your father and your mother, as the LORD your God has commanded you, so that you may live long and that it may go well with you in the land the LORD your God is giving you. (Deuteronomy 5:16 NIV)

~ Cyril Nishimoto, Esq.
www.iwarock.org

ও ঔ ও

There She Is, Miss America

The moment I heard those long-awaited words: "Ladies and gentlemen, here she is—Miss America 1980—Cheryl Prewitt!" I was so happy, happier than I'd ever been in all my life.

"Thank you," I said to the wild, cheering audience. "Oh, thank you, everyone!"

Suddenly, like something from out of a dream, Bert Parks burst into his classic rendition of the Miss America theme song. Red roses and a gleaming scepter were placed in my hands and a sparkling crown upon my head. With a gentle push, I was off and gliding down the lit runway.

This was truly remarkable, considering all that had happened to me, and what God brought me through.

It happened one spring day when I was eleven years old. My sister veered our Chevrolet around a parked car on a two-lane dirt road, a mile from our home in Choctaw County, Mississippi. All of a sudden, an oncoming car came directly at us. I glanced at the other vehicle and noticed it was our neighbors—the Ray family. "God, no!"

Sounds of screeching metal, shattering glass, and screaming rang in my ears.

From the corner of my eye, I watched my sister struggle to

pick up our thirteen-month-old baby brother, who lay limp on the floorboard. Blood covered my sister's face, and her right arm hung at an odd angle.

I tried to move but couldn't. The powerful impact shoved the engine onto my lap and crushed my left leg where I sat pinned in the passenger seat. I hurt everywhere—my back, chest, head, and most of all my leg.

At the hospital, one doctor said, "I can't get all the glass out," as he worked on a 3 ½ inch gash above my right eye.

Another doctor told my dad, "Her leg is a bad break, and I can't say if she'll ever walk again."

Dr. Booth, an old family friend, had taken charge of my case. "Your face had over 100 stitches," the tall, lanky surgeon said to me. "You suffered multiple fractures on your left thigh bone, cuts on your face, and two cracks in your vertebrae."

Two weeks after the accident, everyone had gone home from the hospital but me. I was transferred to another hospital that had one of the best bone specialists in Mississippi, Dr. Sanders. "Your thigh bone is crushed—the largest and strongest bone in the body," he said. "All the little pieces are not aligned properly. I'm going to realign them, insert a pin through your tibia, and put you in a body cast."

I wore a heavy, eighty-pound plaster cast from chest to toe on my left side, and chest to knee on my right. After three of the longest months of my life, it was time for Dr. Booth to remove it. I could hardly contain my excitement.

He sawed off the cast and warned, "It's not a pretty sight."

I looked at my legs and wanted to crawl back into the cast. The top layer of skin had been completely stripped from both legs. My left leg remained weak, limp, and useless. I wondered whether I'd ever walk again.

On a follow-up visit, I said to Dr. Booth, "I still have a constant ache in my supposedly good right knee, with shooting pain that travels from my lower back, hips to mid-spine."

"Your right knee had been badly twisted, and the injury sustained by the back might be a problem for the rest of your life," the surgeon said. "Once you start walking, you'll have to keep an eye on your knee—the joint may go out on you. As far as your back is concerned, well, there's really not much we can do. Hopefully, in time, it'll improve."

The first time I stood for hems, a startling discovery was made. "Your left leg appears about two inches shorter than your right," Mother said.

Immediately we asked the doctors about this. They could only hope it would remedy itself over time. Mother hemmed my clothing to accommodate the difference.

Before returning to school, I prayed. "Thank You God for bringing me this far along in my healing and for increased confidence and mobility. Thanks for all the hope and promise that the coming school year holds."

Classmates vied to carry my books, and everyone wanted to play with my crutches or hear about the accident in gory detail.

The school year passed quickly, and by December I walked but was still severely crippled. The pain in my back remained a problem, and I had chiropractic treatments for six years. One day the doctor wore a glum expression. "I'm afraid there may be a potential problem with your leg."

"Problem?" My voice rose in alarm. "How can there be a problem?"

"Because of the way your injury mended, it's unlikely that you'll ever be able to have children. Your shortened leg has affected your hip alignment. It's something that can't be fixed."

When I returned home Mother asked, "How'd it go?"

I opened my mouth, but the words didn't come out. Instead I burst into tears.

Mother rushed to my side. "Cheryl, what is it?"

I told her what the doctor had said.

"Honey, there's only one thing we can do in a situation like this. We've got to hand this problem over to the Lord. He's the only One who can help."

Mother's comforting words encouraged me. Why was it so difficult for me to believe? "Mother, pray for me. Pray that I'll have faith to believe Jesus can heal me."

"Of course I will. We'll all pray."

Then one day Madelyn, an accomplished pianist and mother of one of my piano students said some encouraging words to me. "There's power in God's Word. Once you believe God can work miracles, your prayers will activate faith— especially when two or more believers come into agreement."

"I've never heard that before. And you've seen it work?"

Madelyn's eyes shone brightly. "Yes, indeed."

For six weeks, I read and studied Bible verses every day, especially chapters where Jesus healed the sick. I listened to teaching tapes and drilled myself on key healing verses and prayed, "Lord, give me the faith to believe You can heal me." I'd find myself thinking and praying about it while working in the garden, babysitting, and practicing my piano. By early autumn, I reached the point where I believed, not only in my head, but deep down in my spirit.

Then one day I attended a healing seminar with Madelyn and her friends. People desiring healing were asked to form a line in front of the large meeting room in Jackson's old Heidelberg Hotel. "Focus your thoughts toward Jesus," the minister said.

I began to pray. "Thank You, Jesus, for loving me. Thank You for healing me. Lord, give me anything and everything You want me to have."

Suddenly the preacher, Brother Kenneth Hagin, was standing before me. "Now, don't think about me. I want you to focus all your thoughts on Jesus." He gently placed his hand on my head. A great sense of security, peace, and confidence surged through me.

"In the name of Jesus . . ." he prayed.

I never heard him finish. Soothing warmth, as though I'd been immersed in a hot tub, enveloped me. I felt overwhelmed, filled to overflowing with God's presence and power, and I basked in His compassion and love. Closing my eyes, I sank to the floor. Someone behind me must have caught me and gently laid me down.

After a while, I sat up and opened my eyes. My legs had been restored to equal length, like two perfectly matched bookends. They're living proof that God in His love and power can take the most crippled legs and transform them into something beautiful. I was healed! "Thank You, Jesus," I whispered. "Oh, thank You!" I wanted to thank the Lord with such a grateful heart that I went right out of English into another beautiful language. I was filled with the Holy Spirit!

Leaping up, I stamped my left foot on the floor over and over to make sure what I'd seen was really true. Each resounding thump was a triumphant affirmation of my healing.

It's because of my God and His truth that I am healed today. He is the reason why I won the pageant, which happened after I began to focus my attention on Him and what I can do for Him.

Today I am a wife, mother, musician, evangelist, and I travel the world with my wonderful husband, bringing people God's message of hope and healing.

"If you abide in Me, and My words abide in you, ask whatever you wish, and it will be done for you." (John 15:7)

~ Cheryl Salem
SalemFamilyMinistries.org

≈ 🕊 ≈

The Strum of Harmony

"Mom, I'm going to check out the guitars at Cripple Creek," Josh said, jingling the van keys.

I dropped the trowel among the tangerine marigolds and straightened. "You need to study!" The staccato words carried a warning. "Your term paper is due Friday."

"Later, Mom. I want to see the guitars first."

Ever since my son turned sixteen, his father and I allowed him to make most of his decisions. I longed to tell him how stupid this was, but I nodded in agreement instead. "Get back soon, so you can finish that paper."

I jabbed the trowel into the dirt and huffed. Why had I agreed to let him make his own choices? He would never earn a college scholarship by fiddling with guitars. I wanted him to do something he loved that paid well, like acoustical engineering.

An hour and a half had passed when the front door closed.

"Mom, I'm back."

"In here."

Josh ambled into the kitchen beaming. "I saw this awesome Gibson that was on sale. I want to get it."

"We'll talk about it later, after your finals. Now, get back to your studies."

He made a face somewhere between a frown and a pout. Then he turned and stomped upstairs.

A week later, I was chopping red peppers for soup when I heard Josh's foot hit the landing. He didn't even glance at me as he pivoted toward the front door. I stiffened. Was he going to ignore study time again?

"Son, what are you up to?"

"I'm headed to Cripple Creek again."

I plunked the knife on the cutting board. "You have four finals next week."

"Oh, Mom, I'll study after."

I pressed my lips together so tightly they hurt. Would it be too heavy-handed to ask for the car keys? I counted to three instead and drew in a deep breath. "Promise me you won't buy anything."

He tossed a "Yeah, right" look in my direction and hurried out the door.

Both the soup and I were simmering when he walked back into the house. When I saw his huge grin and new guitar, my anger shot from hot to scalding. I sucked in air and prepared to hurl flaming words. The rush of adrenaline coursing through my veins surprised and frightened me.

Searching for a better tone, I prayed, "God, give me wisdom." Poised on my toes, body tense, I opened my mouth. Before the words came out, I heard a word that created a deep impression inside me, which halted my furious diatribe.

Stop!

I rocked back on my heels. "Lord, is that you?"

Don't do this. I will use this guitar for My glory.

I stood there, body leaning forward, anger heating my neck and face. "Are you sure, Lord?"

No response.

I relaxed my stance, shook tension from my arms and considered what to do next. My eyes moved from the gleaming guitar to the delight on Josh's face. "Tell me about the guitar, son. Why did you choose this one?"

"Listen." His long, slender fingers strummed across the strings. A well-tuned chord resonated through the room.

"Play another one." The next chord played across my heartstrings, easing tension from my jangled nerves. "I can see why you wanted this one."

"Yeah, Mom, you should hear."

When he finished and headed upstairs to prep for finals, I bowed my head and let out a long sigh. "Lord, thank You so much for stopping my angry words."

If I'd spewed my thoughts, I might have smothered his dream and destroyed our relationship. God had broader plans.

Josh received a college scholarship. When he attended the university, he wrote and performed a song on his Gibson that won the college talent show.

Today Josh is a wise, hard-working, and humble son who leads worship at church and records music for other musicians.

I shudder when I think back at what might have happened if God had not prompted me to pray. Had I lashed out, I would have wounded his spirit and erected a barrier between us. He might have torn me apart with words and raised the wall of bitterness and misunderstanding. Also, I doubt if he would have wanted to come home much after he left for college.

God proved His faithfulness to me and answered with the strum of harmony.

Everyone should be quick to listen, slow to speak and slow to become angry, for man's anger does not bring about the righteous life that God desires (James 1:19-20 NIV)

~ Jinny Sherman

෧ 𝒴 ෨

Beyond Limitations

Mom died in a horrific automobile accident when I was seven, so Dad sent my older brother and me to live with Grandma. The accident left me deaf in my left ear, and another car accident four years earlier had marred my face.

We lived in Mulligan Flats, a poverty-stricken neighborhood in Oklahoma City. Most people lived in unbelievable poverty with a look of hopelessness on their faces.

The home we lived in had a dirt floor that Grandma swept and kept neat. She prayed all the time. I still remember when we ran out of food. Grandma waved me over. "Jesse, come here and pray with me. Ask God to supply our need."

We prayed together, and I sensed God's power flow through the prayer.

The next day Grandma said with excitement, "Your father sent us a check for twenty dollars. Yay, we can buy food!" The prayer made a lasting impression on me.

Not being able to hear well, I suffered from an inferiority complex and learning disabilities. Special education classes for the disabled didn't exist. Teachers didn't know how to help me. So each year they passed me to the next grade, even though I couldn't read or do the lessons.

All that changed in the seventh grade when a teacher failed me. At that point I quit school and went to work. Because of my age and illiteracy, I had limited job opportunities.

My girlfriend, Shirley, began dating me when she turned sixteen. We were married before the year was out, and soon Jesse Jr. was born just two days after my sixteenth birthday.

The first two years of marriage were difficult, and I became very discouraged with the long work hours and low pay. I believed in my heart that I could do better, become an achiever and do something with my life.

When I turned eighteen, my friend Harvey approached me. "How about working with me at the food company?"

"I'm not sure if I could do the work. I don't feel qualified."

"Jesse, you can do anything if you really want to do it."

His words echoed inside me and made a lasting impression on me. "Okay, I'll give it a shot." Everything I achieved came about because I had faith and believed I could be someone special. I chose not to give up on my dreams.

Most of the salesmen lived in nice homes and had a lot of money. After work they stopped off at the clubs and drank a lot. I wanted to be like them. I took an extra job at a convenience store on weekends for a while, so I could drink with them and still have enough to pay the bills. In spite of my illiteracy, I tripled the sales on my route within a year.

Being unable to read was a huge disadvantage in route sales. Many times I stopped in front of street signs and compared the letters to those on my route sheet.

By this time my marriage with Shirley was in shambles, and we were on the verge of divorce. My selfishness, long hours, and drinking drove us apart, while she stayed at home caring for our three children.

Within a few months, the company promoted me to district manager for all of Oklahoma. In that role, I was embarrassed because I couldn't even read a second grade book.

Shirley began to attend church and would invite me, but I'd make up excuses. She rededicated her life to God, and I noticed changes in her. She would be kind to me even when I was unkind to her. I knew something powerful had happened to her, which intrigued me.

Could God make a difference in my life? Finally, I consented to attend a revival service with her.

As the pastor preached, I became disgusted with my lifestyle. *Could God forgive me for all the wrongs I have done? Or the terrible pain I've caused in others?*

When the sermon ended, all I could think about was getting to the altar so I could cry out to God for help.

Something happened to me there, and I left with a spring in my step, and my heart became light and joyful. I knew God had connected with me. A love I never experienced for Shirley filled my heart.

In the grocery stores, people asked, "Is that you, Jesse? What happened to you? You're so different now."

"I received Jesus into my life and His gift of salvation. Why don't you all come to church with Shirley and me?"

Soon, we were bringing over thirty people to church.

Later I attended a Full Gospel Business Men's retreat. During a prayer time, God seemed to be asking me, *Jesse, will you become a preacher of the gospel?*

In my heart I loved God and what He had done for me. I wanted to say yes, but I knew it was beyond my ability.

My desire to read became a driving force, and I sought a tutor.

"Jesse, it amazes me that you're so successful in sales. I know you can learn how to read," said Cindy, my tutor. "Just keep applying yourself."

This is exactly what I need to hear to push myself.

Sometime later, Cindy suggested, "Jesse, you need to attend a university."

"But I haven't even completed high school and never learned how to study. I have no money to attend a university."

Once I agreed to apply, doubts flooded me. What have I agreed to do? How could I think about getting a college degree when I couldn't pass the seventh grade?

To my amazement I was accepted to a university.

That moment, God spoke to me. *This is My work. You could not have gotten into this college or any other if it had not been for Me.*

God's words ignited my faith. If He thought I could do it, then I believed I could too.

The work was hard. Though my professors were patient with my slow reading, they did not cut me any slack. I knew I could barely make the grades to stay in school, but with God's help, I received my diploma. Most of my classmates and school officials knew what I had overcome. On graduation day, I moved my tassel amid a great ovation. That day I knew I could do anything that I really wanted in life.

Receiving my Bachelor of Arts degree was a high pinnacle in my life, as if I conquered the world. But graduate school was next. I continued studying, one semester at a time toward a doctorate. With help from friends to pay the final bill, I walked across the platform one more time as Dr. Jesse Cradduck.

Today Shirley and I bring messages of hope to hurting and needy people at the Family Worship Center City Ministry in Oklahoma City. We also feed the homeless a full meal three nights a week—over fifty thousand meals per year.

Never give up on your dreams.

I can do all things through Christ who strengthens me. (Philippians 4:13 NKJV)

~ Dr. Jesse Cradduck

A Hard Shell

During my childhood, my brother and I attended Dharma School at the San Jose Buddhist Temple, where I later served as president of the Young Buddhist Association. All of my friends were there, and we were a tight-knit group.

I'll never forget the day Mom told us she became a Christian. *How could she betray us?* We're supposed to be Buddhists, just like our grandparents and all the other Japanese Americans we'd grown up with.

Why is Mom forcing me to go to all these Christian events? They raise their hands, jump for joy; some cry and are so into it. I'll just go to make her happy, so she won't give me such a hard time about being with my friends when I'm home from college for winter break.

At one event, a lady to my right whispered, "When you hear Jesus knock, don't harden your heart."

Who was she? I didn't know her. Why was she talking to me? Good thing my best friend, Jen, came with me. We kept exchanging odd glances at each other.

In the Buddhist temple, I enjoyed the practical teachings of self-control, discipline, and meditation that had understandable examples. We learned to control our own destiny and outcome.

"Forget all of that. God controls everything," Mom said, Not having any control over anything didn't exactly put my mind at ease.

On another day Mom said, "Shannon, you're physically alive, but spiritually dead—"

"Leave me alone!" I screamed. "Mom, I know you believe in Jesus, but that doesn't mean I have to believe what you believe. I need to make my own decisions. Besides, why would I want to become a Christian? They're hypocrites. Those weird Christian students in that club on campus, they close their eyes, hold hands, and pray in the middle of the main walkway. Don't they care that people are looking at them?"

Mom looked at me with sad eyes.

I continued ranting. "Two men walk around my college campus with their big signs and ridiculous hats, claiming just about everyone is going to hell. They yell at everyone who walks by. Then another guy argues with them, saying they aren't preaching from the Bible. Can someone please make up their mind?"

Several months later, Mom handed me a gift from her friend. "Mrs. Hiura gave you this book to read."

I glanced at the cover. Lee Strobel's *The Case for Christ: A Journalist's Personal Investigation of the Evidence for Jesus.*

"Oh, great. Another Christian book."

These nice people keep wasting their money on me. Why is it so important to them that I believe in God? They must think I'm such a deviant. I'm actually a really nice and giving person. I just don't understand the whole Jesus thing.

Why can't I just be a good person without being a Christian? Not all people who believe in Jesus are perfect, so what makes them different than me? Hey, don't sin, but if you do, Jesus will forgive you. Well, isn't that like a free ticket to do whatever you want? That's no standard to live by. It feels like a get-out-of-jail freebie, and they still can feel reassured about whatever they do. Christianity is for the weak who can't handle life on their own.

Hopefully this book will be more intriguing than the last one, about how sex before marriage is immoral. Don't these people have anything good to say? It's always about: if you do this or if you do that, you're a sinner. So, you mean I have the chance to join a religion that constantly reminds me that I'm not perfect, and I get to feel guilty about everything every day for the rest of my life? *Awesome, where do I sign up?*

Mom would keep bugging me to read this, so I decided to take a look at least. I opened the book and fanned through the pages. *Hmm, this book is written from a scientific standpoint. Something I can relate to—hard evidence.*

I began reading the book, and surprisingly, I couldn't put it down. So many thoughts ran through my mind. Why was I so opposed to the whole Jesus thing? What was I afraid of? What if I was wrong and Jesus did exist? Then I was definitely on my way to hell. What do I have to lose? I think I'd rather give myself a chance at going to heaven than not.

"Mom, I finished the book."

"You did? What did you think of it?"

"For once, I'm impressed. The author is just like me. He needed evidence to believe in Jesus. He went through great lengths to interview people, scientists, and researchers to disprove Jesus's existence.

After his exhaustive research, he couldn't disprove anything. It has me thinking."

"Good. I want you to meet with Pastor Jim Sakurai on your trip home from school next weekend. He can answer some of your questions better than I can."

When I met with Pastor Sakurai, I was ready to receive Jesus. I didn't know what to expect and was a little nervous. He led me in a simple prayer, and I accepted Christ into my life—nothing to be afraid of at all.

About one month later, 911 changed our world. I was back at college in San Diego, watching everything on TV. Heart pounding, I began to pray. "Jesus, I'm so scared. Maybe this military town is a target too. Why is this all happening?" I went to bed that evening with so many thoughts in my head, but God's peace filled me after praying, and I fell asleep.

I slowly gave up on the belief that I had to be in control of everything. It definitely was a struggle to let Jesus into my life, since I had a lot of pride.

Over time, I've seen things occur that could only be God's work, for no alternative explanations fit. Sometimes I can physically feel something in my heart. I know it's Jesus talking straight to my soul.

I'm still growing in my faith, and I have my faults, but God accepts me and continues to work with me.

It took a while to get through my stubborn ways and out of my hard shell. I'm grateful to discover Jesus is a real person and the living God.

He who has the Son has life; he who does not have the Son of God does not have life. (1 John 5:12 NKJV)

~ Shannon Sakamoto, Ed.D.

ॡ ৺ ৵

How to Stop a Train

My husband gave our daughter a hug and leaned over to kiss me. Our other child clung to my hip, waving bye-bye.

"Have a good day," I said as usual. The three of us stayed in the warm sunshine on the porch, blowing kisses and waving until the blue one-ton pickup turned the corner. "Come on. Let's eat." I hitched the one up a bit on my hip and herded the other down the corridor into the kitchen.

Elizabeth crawled into the booster seat like a big girl. I settled Chipper into the high chair and gave him a spoon to thump on the tray while I filled the breakfast bowls. Once the milk was poured, the cereal snapped, crackled, and popped. I sat down.

Automatically, my daughter folded her hands and bowed her head. I stilled Chipper's tiny hands between mine. "Thank You, Jesus, for this food. Help us be good today," I prayed.

Elizabeth's head came up, and Chipper reached for his Nestle's Quik bunny mug.

"And keep Daddy safe." I added. The clink of spoons on bowls and the happy chatter of precocious kids resumed.

An hour later I shook hot soapy bubbles from my hands and hurried to answer the insistent, ringing phone. "Hello?"

A calm and collected voice asked, "Are you Mary Allen?"

"Yes."

"Mrs. Allen, this is the hospital. Your husband was in an accident this morning, and you need to come to the emergency room for him."

"Okay," I answered with calm equal to the caller's. "I'll be there as soon as I can."

I dialed my mother-in-law and arranged to drop the children at her house.

"There's nothing to worry about," I assured her. "They said to come pick him up because his vehicle was smashed."

Once the kids were with Grandma, I sped into town, anxious to be with John, but I was not worried about him.

The emergency room was full. Babies cried, people coughed, and the overhead PA called for a doctor to report to a certain room. A nurse took me aside and whispered, "Your husband was hit by a train this morning."

"Wha-at? Is he okay?" In our community, I knew of men, women, and children who had been hit by a train and died.

"He's in X-ray now. We'll know more later—whether he can walk again."

Fear crowded my mind. What if he died? What if he were permanently disabled? How would we survive?

The nurse directed me to a bed being pushed down the hall. John lay facedown with a sheet over his body. A large foam brace immobilized his neck. I followed as they wheeled him into a curtained area.

"John, are you in pain?"

"I'm okay."

"They said the train hit you."

"You know where the road is a Y over the tracks?"

I knew the place. No crossing guards or blinking lights give warning at that remote site. Woods and tall brush extend in both directions, making visibility difficult.

"I edged onto the tracks to look for the train, and it was right there. Then all I saw was the R on the gear shaft. I didn't even have time to shift before the train slammed into me. It spun me around, caught the rear and bounced me out of the way. The truck is a total loss and looks like your accordion. The back almost touches the front. When the ambulance arrived, the paramedics made me wear this neck brace."

Aluminum whispered against aluminum as the privacy curtains brushed aside. A doctor entered and greeted us. He had John turn onto his back as he examined him. The bed whirred to an upright position. The doctor pulled the Velcro fastener, releasing the neck brace.

"Is he paralyzed?"

"No. We can find nothing wrong, no broken bones, no swelling, no internal injuries, and certainly no paralysis. A little bruising, but blood work and X-rays appear normal."

"He's okay?"

"Yes, he's fine. We don't know how he survived, let alone without injury."

I recalled the nudging to pray for his safety. "I do. That crossing is five minutes from home. That's the exact time I prayed for his safety."

I stood in awe thinking about what could have happened. With a grateful heart, I thanked God for protecting John.

Many *are* the afflictions of the righteous, but the LORD delivers him out of them all. He guards all his bones; not one of them is broken. (Psalm 34:19–20 NKJV)

~ Mary Allen

The Promise

The carpenter foreman rushed into my work area. "Hey, Bernal, there's an emergency call for you in the office."

I hurried over there and grabbed the phone.

"Carla's back in the hospital for profuse hemorrhaging," my wife's sister, Karen, shrilled.

"I'll be right there." I hung up and flew out of the office.

Carla had just given birth to Sarah a few days earlier. Now, she had complications just like her mother who died giving birth to her. Heart pounding, I tried to calm myself.

The 90-mile ride from Sacramento to Paradise, California, seemed like a million miles long. Choice words flew from my mouth. I slammed my fist against the dashboard and floored the accelerator. It felt like I was crawling, even at 100 mph.

Here I was a drinking, smoking, cursing heathen who ran around with the Hell's Angels, but my God-fearing, Bible-reading wife was bleeding to death.

"It's not fair!" I ranted. "That God of hers!"

I ran every red light and trembled when the hospital came into view.

Who designed this thing called life? If God's in charge, why do people suffer?

If I prayed for Carla, would God even listen?

At my wits end, I quit thinking and started praying. "God, Jesus, Whoever You are, please help Carla. I beg You, please heal my wife. She truly loves You and talks about You to me. I know I don't deserve an audience with You, but if You can find it in Your heart to do this, I will do whatever You want. I will. I promise. Thank You for hearing me out."

I double-parked and hurtled into the emergency entrance.

The doctor stepped out of Carla's room. "Dick, we've got a major problem. A piece of the placenta was not expelled after the delivery. When it broke loose, it tore a main artery. We can't seem to stop the hemorrhaging." He sighed. "We've already done a dilation and curettage procedure. Now we're thinking of a complete hysterectomy."

Carla looked like a corpse—yellow skin and chalk-white lips. Nurses worked frantically to get her blood pressure up, but it kept dropping. She whispered, "I'm sorry, honey."

I patted Carla's soft blonde hair. "What are you sorry for? It's not your fault. Don't worry; you're going to be fine."

Visiting hours were over, so I drove to her sister, Karen's home. She was looking after Sarah. When I arrived, I cuddled little Sarah in a rocking chair. "Your mom is in a bit of a jam right now. I wish I could be as peaceful as you."

Every time the phone rang, I flinched. I wanted to answer it, yet I feared the worst. News spread to family and friends. Many offered help, money, and even their own blood.

Finally the doctor called. "We're going to decide on the hysterectomy in the morning."

The next day, Karen and I anxiously waited outside Carla's room. I repeated my promise to God.

The doctor emerged from Carla's room with a bright smile. "We seem to have some kind of miracle. Last night, the blood flow suddenly stopped. I can't explain it, but I can tell you that we have a young woman who is rapidly recovering."

I raced into her room. My wife was sitting up, and eating Jell-O. I threw my arms around her. "What a relief."

Later that day, while walking across the parking lot, I gazed at the sky and said aloud, "Thank You, God."

Wow, that felt good. Then I remembered my impulsive promise: If You will heal Carla, I will do anything You ask of me. What on earth can God do with me? Nothing. I'm not in His league. I shuffled on.

Three days later, Carla was released from the hospital.

For the next several weeks, I tried to get back into my usual routine, but I kept thinking about God. *Who is He anyway?* I caught myself staring at the sky and wondering about the place called heaven.

Then one clear day toward the end of duck season, I sat watching the geese and ducks migrate south. *Why do they do that? Is there really a God who controls nature? Amazing!*

Hmm, where do I fit in?

"Carla dear, I'm going to the club in the morning. It's the last week of duck season. But I'll come home tomorrow night, and we can go to church Sunday morning."

Her eyes grew wide. "Really? Honest? Oh, honey, that's great! God finally answered my prayers."

I hope she understands that I'm not going to make it a habit. I just wanted to make good on my promise to God and show up once in church.

Carla rededicated her life to Jesus after we went to church. She dropped an odd-looking book called *Wordless* into my lap. Inside were colored pages.

Black represents man's life without God.

Gold symbolizes God's purity and holiness.

Red signifies the blood of Jesus that takes away our sins.

White represents sins cleansed by the blood of Jesus.

I read the book, and it made sense to me. I made a decision to receive Jesus into my heart and prayed the little prayer for salvation: "Dear God, I acknowledge I have followed my own way and that I am a sinner. I ask You to forgive me. Please accept me into Your family and guide me all the days of my life. In Jesus's name, amen."

A heavy weight lifted off of me, and a deep freedom and happiness enveloped me.

When Carla discovered I had received Jesus, she burst into tears, jumped up and down, and clapped her hands.

About a year later, a voice spoke to me while I was driving to work. I couldn't tell if it was audible or deep within me.

Dick, prepare yourself for service, for I have called you.

I looked around. "Who said that?" I turned my head and didn't see anyone. No one was there. A shiver ran down my spine. "Lord, is that You?"

The voice came again. *Dick, prepare yourself for service, for I have called you.*

"Okay, Lord." My willingness to obey surprised me. God led me to quit my high-paying job and attend Bible college. After graduating, I sensed the Lord calling me to start a church. It began small with just my family and a few friends.

Today, it has grown into a very large church with thousands of people—all nationalities and backgrounds. I praise God for this amazing work He has done.

God demonstrates His own love toward us, in that while we were still sinners, Christ died for us. (Romans 5:8 NKJV)

~ Dick Bernal, founder, Jubilee Christian Center
www.jubilee.org

The Oil of Joy for Mourning

Where could I find peace when I felt so alone?

I stirred out of deep sleep into the first glimmer of a new day and flung my arm as usual to my husband's side of the bed.

He wasn't there.

With a jolt I came fully awake, the pain knifing through my heart with the knowledge that he would never sleep beside me again. He had died five days ago, and while I was at peace that he was celebrating his new life in heaven, I was still fastened to this earth, and I certainly didn't feel like celebrating the separation. To be the one left here is the more difficult part.

I moved through the morning like a zombie. The memorial service was over and the out-of-town family members had left. The day looked like a bleak, dreary desert, while the emptiness of the house reflected the emptiness within me.

I once heard someone say losing a spouse was like losing an arm or leg. God joined the two of us in marriage and said, "The two have become one." I still had two arms and two legs, but my whole interior seemed to be missing, as though I had been hollowed out.

In the afternoon, I sat on the patio and stared at the garden. In the center of a spread of scarlet penstemon and blue columbine stood the birdbath our children had given us on our 50th wedding anniversary. The stone raccoon perched on it peered back at me with saucy eyes, reminding me of Bob's encounter with a live raccoon the summer before. Pink blooms blanketed the nearby nectarine tree that Bob had grown from a seed, which promised delicious fruit in the summer. Blossoms sprinkled the grass beneath it, the topmost branches stretched to the sky, sharing their beauty with the earth below.

I sighed and retreated into the house. My heart couldn't accept the beauty yet. Inside or outside, reminders of my husband were everywhere I looked: his woodworking skills with a knickknack shelf, his favorite chair, the coffee cup he'd bought for me and often brought to me when I was working, filled with coffee fixed the way I like it. Only one thing was missing—Bob himself.

We'd been a close couple for more than 50 years of marriage, sharing the bumpy and smooth stretches and growing together. Our former closeness made his absence more painful.

Desperately longing to feel his arms around me, I went to the coat closet and hugged his down jacket that still held a whiff of his aftershave. My tears made spots on the nylon, and I knew the jacket was only a poor substitute, but after a few minutes I calmed down and closed the closet door.

Then I caught sight of the item that had more to say about Bob than the house, yard, or his clothes: his Bible. He'd been a minister for more than 25 years and loved that Bible from front cover to back.

He believed it was all the Word of God, and even in his last days quoted it, discussed it, and wanted it read to him. I believed it too, and putting my hand on it, was comforted by knowing it was real and unchanging, as is God Himself.

The foremost priority in our lives was the spiritual well-being of our family and those Bob ministered to over the years. The Word of God was always the focus for prayer, praise, and counseling. If I had a question or concern, the "answer man" was somewhere in the house or yard. Now, that man was unavailable to me for conversation of any kind.

Instead my first words each day became "Good morning, Father." I couldn't hear His spoken words in return, but reading his Word gave me comfort and also answers.

Renewing my joy, being reminded of God's incredible love, and knowing His peace that is beyond understanding were all waiting for me to rediscover by opening the Bible.

God gives us tears to heal. I didn't enjoy the times I was taken unaware by sudden sobbing, but it was a healthy step. Even through my tears, I was aware of God's love surrounding me. Laughter is another healing tool. I didn't think I'd be able to laugh again, but eventually laughter returned. And always, God's loving presence was real.

Being alone in the house felt downright creepy at times. Sometimes I awoke to vague sounds, cracks, rattles, and indescribable noises. Was someone walking stealthily through the house? Was someone trying to break through a window? Worst of all, was I losing my faith? Then God in His infinite love and patience reminded me that He never sleeps, and His arms were still around me to shelter and protect me.

I had often heard the words, "I will never leave you nor forsake you" (Hebrews 13:5 NKJV). Now, I needed to apply those words and reach out to God with all my heart and soul, knowing His love surrounded me, no matter where I was. My house was not empty. God filled it. I did not drive by myself— He rode with me every mile. This realization sank in, and as the days passed, I was comforted and strengthened, even to the point of an astounding joy. And I was no longer afraid.

I knew I needed to get on with my life. My first priority was returning to church. Because I stayed home as a caregiver during Bob's illness, I had missed months of worshiping with my church family. God certainly doesn't limit His presence to church—I knew that. But I needed the fellowship of the congregation and the joy of worshiping together. Another important step was to keep busy. Some things had been neglected during the past months, but one day at a time, one step at a time, was the best I could do.

When I woke from sleep I still reached over to Bob's side of the bed. When I walked into the house after being away, I still looked to see where he was. I wondered if I was going to do this the rest of my life. Sometimes I felt confused as if waking from a dream. Had this really happened? Was he really dead? Then I would remember with a new sorrow; yes, he's gone.

I had peace because I had perfect confidence that Bob was in heaven. Heaven is a real place, and I know Bob is there right now in the presence of God, kneeling before His throne. He is praising God and worshiping with crowds of saints who have gone before him into the Holy One's presence. He is seeing Jesus face-to-face, marveling at the wonder of Him, and in awe of His majesty. I will see Bob again when I step out of this world and into heaven.

Because I love God, I want to please Him in everything. Serving Him is my calling, and to serve Him I must serve others. By doing this I bring Him praise and glory.

By going through the loneliness that had at times engulfed me, so I could hardly move or breathe, I could understand when other women go through that despairing feeling. God allowed me to endure that and patiently waited until I had acknowledged by faith that He was ever-present.

I talked about that presence to other women living alone and began to pray for others around the world. I asked God to help them see that they were loved not only by Him, but by me also, an unknown someone who cares.

God is still on His throne. His Word, His love, His grace, and His care of us have never changed and never will change.

No matter how many days or years I have to walk without my husband, I am not really alone. I know now the amazing joy I experience is the awareness of my Father who completely surrounds me and makes His presence known to me.

God has always been with me, but now I am fully convinced of it and can really rejoice and praise Him. He'll never leave me.

Even through my tears, God's love surrounded me.

You keep track of all my sorrows. You have collected all my tears in your bottle. (Psalm 56:8 NLT)

~ Shirley Shibley, Freelance writer
Glendora, California

"The Oil of Joy for Mourning," *THE LOOKOUT*, August 7, 2005. Used by permission.

~ 𝓨 ~

Korean Hope

The audience rose from their seats and loud applause reverberated throughout the vast auditorium at Cape Town's Convention Centre in South Africa, shortly after Choi Yong Ja,* the daughter of a former high-ranking government leader in North Korea, finished telling her story.

The petite, eighteen-year-old let out a graceful smile and talked about being an only child of a very wealthy family in Pyongyang, the capital of North Korea. Her father had served as an assistant to Kim Jong-il—the leader of the country.

When Yong Ja was six years old, the North Korean government persecuted their family for political reasons, so they escaped to China in 1998. After settling there, a relative invited them to a Christian church, and her parents came to know the amazing grace and love of God.

A few months later, her mother, who was pregnant with her second child, died of leukemia. In the midst of this great tragedy, her father started a Bible study with missionaries from South Korea and America. He had a burning desire to become a missionary to his native country in North Korea.

In 2001 the Chinese police reported him and arrested him. They sent him back to North Korea, forcing him to leave Yong

Ja behind. He was sentenced to three years in prison. Rather than complain or blame God, he cried out to Him desperately. The incarceration served only to strengthen his faith.

Her father returned to China after being released from prison, and he reunited briefly with his daughter. He chose not to go to South Korea where he could enjoy religious freedom. Instead he gathered Bibles and returned to North Korea to share Christ's message of life and hope among the hopeless people of his homeland.

In 2006 his work was discovered by the government, and he was once again imprisoned.

Choking back tears, Yong Ja says, "It breaks my heart that I have heard no word from my father nor information about him ever since. In all probability, he has been shot to death in public on charges of treason and espionage, as is often the case for persecuted Christians in North Korea.

"At the time of my father's first arrest, I wasn't a Christian. A young Chinese pastor's family adopted me and showed me great love and care. But the pastor and his wife had to go to America in 2007. Shortly after that, I was given the opportunity to go to South Korea. While waiting to go there, I stayed at the Korean embassy in Beijing when something unusual happened.

"Late one night, I saw Jesus in a dream. He had tears in His eyes. He walked toward me and said, 'Choi Yong, how much longer are you going to keep Me waiting? Walk with Me. Yes, you lost your earthly father, but I am your Heavenly Father, and whatever has happened to you was because I love you.'

"I awoke from the dream, assured that God loved and cared about me so much He sent His Son Jesus to die for me. I knelt down by my bed and prayed to God for the first time. 'God, here I am. I just lay down everything and give you my heart, my soul, my mind, and my strength. Please use me as you will.'"

Looking out over the audience, Yong Ja adds, "I look back at my short life—six years in North Korea, eleven years in China, and one year in South Korea—and I see God's hand everywhere."

God placed a deep love in her heart for North Korea like her father. She says, "I now desire to be obedient to God. I want to bring the love of Jesus to North Korea.

"All the sadness and grief I suffered, everything I learned and experienced, I want to give it all to God and use my life for His kingdom. I hope to honor my father and bring glory to my Heavenly Father by serving God with my whole heart.

"I'm preparing to get into the university to study political science and diplomacy. Then I want to return to North Korea and work with my people whose rights have been taken away.

"In closing, I humbly ask you, my brothers and sisters, to have the same heart of God. Please pray that the same light of God's grace and mercy that reached my father, mother, and now me, will come down on the people of North Korea."[1]

It's because of people like Yong Ja, there is hope for North Korea—a country that's been divided from the South since World War II, with families split apart. I look forward to the day God answers those prayers for North Korea.

"If you abide in My word, you are My disciples indeed. And you shall know the truth, and the truth shall make you free." (John 8:31–32 NKJV)

~ Adapted by Gail Kaku for Choi Yong Ja

[1] Cape Town, South Africa, October 2010 - The Third Lausanne Congress. Used by Permission. *Names have been changed to protect privacy.

❧ 𝕏 ❧

I Was a Kamikaze Pilot

My mother gave me a stern look. "Don't come back alive. I expect you to fulfill your duty and fight for the emperor."

Although I'm a Japanese American who grew up in Oregon, my family and I were living in Japan when World War II broke out. I had just graduated from high school and was drafted into the Imperial Japanese Navy. It was either that or prison. So I "volunteered" to become a kamikaze pilot.

I'm American, but part of me is Japanese. It was my duty to die in this war and obey my mother. Most of all I was in Japan, not America.

I underwent rigorous aircraft training for sixteen months in Yokaiden. One exercise included sitting in a barber-like chair, being spun around about fifty times and then standing at attention for three minutes. If we couldn't withstand the G-force, we were kicked out of the program.

During a training flight, I rolled and pitched the plane and soared like an eagle whipping through some very strong winds. I looked down and could see people moving about. We made our descent through the clouds, and the landing gear smoothly made contact with the earth.

"Where'd you learn to fly like that? You're doing real

well," my instructor sitting behind me asked in Japanese.

"I took glider training in high school." The instructor treated me really well after that. I quickly accumulated more than twenty hours of flight time and passed all of the tests.

The first three months the commander gave all kamikaze pilots cigarettes, liquor—whatever we asked for. We ate the finest foods and enjoyed chocolates at night.

We were treated like kings and wore impressive button-down uniforms having distinctive wings on both shoulders with blue cherry blossom insignia, differentiating us from medics, who wore white insignia, and mechanics, black ones.

During the winter, we dressed in pure-white wool uniforms. Every Sunday the high school girls waited for us at the gate. We usually went to the movies with them.

Every three months we were transferred to a different place, drawing closer to our final destination of Okinawa. At this time, the war was getting really bad, and we were being transferred to Fukuoka.

Oh boy, that's near my parents' home.

On the way over there, the train rumbled through smoldering towns and flattened cities. Dead bodies were piled up like mountains and were being burned.

Every time the train stopped at a station, crowds of people flocked around us, begging, "Please give us *gohan* [rice]."

I felt sick to my stomach seeing so many dead bodies and starving people.

Our next stop was Kagoshima, then on to the battle of Okinawa. Mom's words echoed inside me. *Don't come back alive.* A chill cascaded down my spine.

Some kamikaze pilots tucked love notes into bottles and dropped them by their homes before crashing their planes. One person wrote: *Father, Mother, I don't want to die.*

The commander made an announcement. "There's a change of plans. We're out of planes and fuel."

Through the network of kamikaze pilots, I had heard five-thousand of them plunged their planes into American ships—some succeeded; many were shot down by anti-aircraft fire and plummeted into the sea.

The commander held up a long object. "This is a stick bomb. Your new mission is to camouflage yourselves, roll underneath an enemy tank, and blow it up."

Just before we boarded the train, the commander paced up and down the line. "Anybody know English?"

The person behind me pointed at me. "This guy is from America."

The commander called me over. "I need you to translate leaflets the American bombers are dropping."

Everyone left for the mission except me. I immediately began translating the material containing U.S. military warnings of air raids on major cities.

Several weeks later, the atomic bombs fell on Hiroshima and Nagasaki, and Japan finally surrendered.

Many citizens couldn't believe Japan had lost. The captain who trained the kamikaze pilots went to an open field and committed *hara-kiri*—jabbing himself in the stomach with a sword and moving the blade across and upward.

After the war, I returned to my parents' home in Kokura. Mom opened the door and gasped. She threw her arms around me and hugged me. "I'm so happy to see you alive!" Her words melted me. *She didn't want me to die after all.*

I stayed in Japan for several years and worked as a translator in the American military at Camp Kokura.

When I returned to America, my sister and I went back to our parents' home in Oregon where strangers were now living. At the gas station, we ran into one of the caretakers who used to look after our farm. "They took everything away—your parents' house, farm, horses—all their possessions." He didn't know exactly who "they" were.

I moved out of state, worked odd jobs and eventually got married. We settled down in the San Francisco Bay Area.

Another couple visited us regularly. "We'd like you to be our guests at a Japanese Christian church?"

"No! We're Buddhists."

However, they didn't give up. "We've noticed your little girl, Susan, doesn't walk well. Can we pray for her?"

The request sounded strange, but we had nothing to lose. They prayed for Susan and to our amazement, God healed her. We had never seen a miracle before, and this prompted us to attend their church.

Gradually I understood that Christianity is a personal relationship with God through His Son, Jesus, who saves people from sin and offers eternal life in heaven. Buddhism is a man-made religion in which people strive for perfection through their own efforts.

Eventually my wife and I accepted Jesus into our hearts, and our lives began to change when we joined a Bible study and fellowship group.

I am thankful God spared me from the suicide missions. Life is too precious to be thrown away like that. Had I died in my sins, I would have suffered an eternity without Him. I believe God preserved my life so I can live a meaningful life serving Him and introducing others to Him.

See to it that no one takes you captive through hollow and deceptive philosophy, which depends on human tradition and the basic principles of this world rather than on Christ. (Colossians 2:8 NIV)

~ Jimmie Matsuda

æ ¥ ∂

Unfathomable

KaBOOM! I was diving out of a moving truck, performing a stunt for a TV show *Airwolf* when the truck suddenly burst into flames. The massive fire explosion knocked me out. My entire face, neck, and arms received life-threatening second- and third-degree burns. The blast also tore off my upper lip.

The medical personnel shot me full of morphine and wrapped my face in bandages as I moaned in agony. I fought for my life and clung to my favorite healing scriptures and meditated on them around the clock.

Earlier that week, my beeper had gone off for a one-day job for a show I sometimes worked on. It paid five hundred dollars—a lot of money back in the 1980s for a Hollywood stuntwoman.

God spoke to my spirit. *Never work on that show again.*

"No, no, no. I want this job. This looks really exciting, and it's a great opportunity." Money had been the hook in my jaw.

Now with my face burned off, I wondered what amount of money was worth this. Certainly not five-hundred dollars. Certainly not a million. I wouldn't take a billion dollars.

The first few days at the Sherman Oaks Burn Center, I couldn't lift a leg or talk much. All I could do was lie still.

It dawned on me that God wasn't trying to withhold a blessing from me by saying "No" to the job. He wanted to protect me. He had my absolute best interest in mind. The devil who comes to kill, steal, and destroy wanted to take my life that day.

When my husband, Mel, visited me at the hospital, he read the Bible to me. So much peace and life filled my heart.

My situation required more than prayer. People graciously prayed and fasted for me. Many friends visited me. One person brought me a *Glamour* magazine. *How funny, now that I don't have a face.* I didn't want to look at these beautiful girls.

My precious husband brought old pictures of me working on shows like *The Dukes of Hazard, Remington Steele*, and *The Fall Guy*. I made a conscious decision not to look in the mirror.

When the nurses swung by, they would say, "It's time to adjust to the way you look now."

"No!" I chose to look at the pictures Mel put up.

One of the greatest difficulties I had as a burn victim was my healing skin sticking to the bandages. When the staff removed them, new skin pulled off with green puss. Then they'd scrape the bloody wound to clean it. The pain was excruciating!

"Please, take me off all painkillers," I said to the staff. "They're giving me an allergic reaction and making me vomit. I am going to believe God will help me."

Despite the enormous pain, I slowly began to recover. I continued meditating upon healing scriptures.

By the fourth day, I walked.

One day I soaked the bandages in the shower so my skin wouldn't stick to them. Yet, the bandages wouldn't come off. I shut off the water and dropped to my knees and wept before God. "This is so painful. This is not fun. I shouldn't be here. Just a week ago, everything was fine." I caught myself wallowing in self-pity.

"Oh Lord, I'm sorry. I know You don't hear us when we complain, but You dwell among our praises." I began to praise and worship God, right there on my knees.

"Lord, I thank You that You've taken sin and diseases upon Your body when You died for us. Thank You for being my Creator, for designing and loving me. Also thanks for being my Healer and Savior. You can fix any problem, any hurt—"

All of a sudden, the tangible presence of God showed up and encompassed me with overwhelming peace and deep love. I sat on my knees and looked down. All of my bandages were neatly on the ground—nothing on my face.

"Lord, You've given me this amazing breakthrough, just minutes after I shifted my focus from my pity party on to You. Even though I messed up, You fixed my situation. I completely disobeyed You, and I know disobeying is huge. But You still loved me and taught me so much through this experience."

Ten days later I was released from the hospital. My doctor said, "Desiree, this is beyond medical recovery. It must be your faith in God that healed you."

New skin grew back on my face without any scarring, and God miraculously healed me.

He turned my tragic situation into a multitude of blessings. Now I'm invited all over the country to talk about my story and minister healing to people.

Give attention to my words; incline your ear to my sayings. Do not let them depart from your sight; keep them in the midst of your heart. For they are life to those who find them and health to all their body. (Proverbs 4:20–22)

~ Desiree Ayres, Cofounder, In His Presence Church
www.ihpchurch.org

࿐ 🕊 ࿐

Arms Wide Open

My husband, Lance,* rarely talks about patients in his surgical practice, but one day he came home clearly agitated.

"I saw a patient today who's in his fifties but can easily pass for his thirties," he said over dinner. "He's in great shape—lifts weights and swims one hundred laps regularly."

"Why did he need to see you?"

"He had a lump in his groin area. I did a biopsy a week ago, and the results showed cancer."

"Oh, no," was all I could say. This brought back painful memories of my father who died of cancer when I was a child.

"That's not the worst of it. I operated on him today, but the cancer has spread throughout his body. I had to tell him he doesn't have long to live."

"I wonder how the patient feels."

Lance paused then spoke again. "I feel led to pray for him. Maybe God will heal him. Will you go with me to visit him?"

I hesitated, then agreed at his unusual request.

On Saturday afternoon, we arrived at the patient's home. His wife, Yasmin,* a lovely woman with dark wavy hair, greeted us. "Thank you so much for coming over." She ushered us into their family room, where a mobile bed had been placed.

Her husband, Scott,* was sitting up in bed, facing the garden by a window where sunlight seeped in. He turned his head and greeted us with a bigger-than-life smile. "Hi, Dr. Liu,* thanks for coming over. You must be Mrs. Liu." He extended his hand and shook mine vigorously.

Lance made small, polite talk with Scott as I surveyed the room. Then he asked Scott, "Do you believe Jesus is God, and He has the power to heal you?"

"I believe Jesus is God, but I think there are many gods. It's narrow-minded to believe there is only one god."

"I see. Rachel and I believe in Jesus as the *only* God. That is why we came to pray *only* in His name for your physical healing."

"I appreciate it." Scott stretched his arms out. "I want to believe Jesus is the only God, but He'll have to prove it to me."

Lance and I laid hands on Scott and prayed aloud for him to be healed in Jesus's name.

When we finished praying, Scott flashed a boyish grin and crossed his muscular arms. "Thanks for praying for me."

My husband returned the smile. "Do you mind if we stop by again and see how God answers our prayers?"

"I would love it. Come as often as you can."

We continued visiting Scott and were optimistic that his health would improve. Perhaps Jesus would heal Scott so he would believe Jesus is the *only* God.

But Scott's health continued to deteriorate. The disease wasted his once muscular body to such a feeble state that he became bedridden.

"Other patients would have died by now," Lance said. "I think God is keeping Scott alive for a reason."

I pictured Scott's hollowed face and pencil-like arms. "I don't know why Jesus hasn't answered our prayers."

In Scott's presence, we tried to stay upbeat and confident, but my faith faltered.

"Have you considered who Jesus is?" we asked.

"I just want you to pray for me," he answered.

On another occasion, a group of people chanted in their living room. "Who are they?" we asked Yasmin.

"Buddhist monks. Scott welcomes their prayers as well."

I was deflated. *Jesus, where are You? Aren't you going to show us You're the real God?*

Then one day Yasmin called. "Scott is unresponsive. The hospice nurse said he is going to die soon." She cried in waves of hysteria. "Please come and pray for him."

After discussing it with Lance, we visited that night and brought our friend Grant.* Before stepping out of the car, we prayed. "Please be with us, Jesus. We need You to be present."

Scott was unconscious and unresponsive to us.

Oh, no! It's too late.

In a calm but authoritative voice, Lance declared, "In the name of Jesus, I command you to wake up. Come out of your stupor so you will hear what we have to say."

Instantly, Scott woke up and squeezed Yasmin's hand, letting us know he could hear us.

"Scott, are you ready to go into the arms of Jesus?" *Where did those words come from? Did God put them in my head?*

Yasmin shook her head. "He didn't squeeze my hand. Please keep it simple."

Grant drew closer to Scott. "Do you believe in Jesus?"

She smiled. "He squeezed my hand!"

"Scott, will you receive Jesus into your heart right now?" Grant asked.

A few seconds passed. Yasmin announced with delight, "He squeezed my hand again!"

Grant opened his Bible and read the following verse:

"But as many as received Him, to them He gave the right to become children of God." (John 1:12)

Driving home, we rejoiced about Scott's acceptance of Jesus. Yet I was skeptical. He had rejected Jesus so many times. How could I be sure he's saved?

The next day Scott passed away. Lance and I visited Yasmin that evening and offered our condolences.

While she sat with us, she said with excitement, "Listen, something amazing happened this morning. My friend showed up at the door with a basket of cookies. I hadn't talked to her for a long time, and she didn't know Scott was dying.

"You wouldn't believe what she said to me. 'Yasmin, I had a dream last night. Jesus was standing in the field with His arms wide open, and Scott was running to Him.'"

My mouth dropped open. "I remembered my last words to him. 'Scott are you ready to go into the arms of Jesus?' Wow, Scott running to Jesus? And Jesus had His arms wide open?"

Then it dawned on me that Jesus *had* heard our prayers. He had been waiting all along for Scott to accept Him. And when he did, Jesus received him into Heaven.

This showed me how much Jesus loved Scott. He didn't have to spend a lifetime earning God's love. All he had to do was say, "Yes" even if it was minutes before he died.

Salvation is found in no one else, for there is no other name under heaven given to men by which we must be saved. (Acts 4:12 NIV)

~ Rachel Liu*

* Names have been changed to protect privacy.

❧ 🕊 ☙

Unstoppable

My doctor told me, "Mr. Silvoso, you have at most two years to live."

I remember that day vividly.

The doctor reached for a piece of chalk and drew a horizontal line on the blackboard. "This line represents your health now. You are tenuously holding your own. However, anytime in the next two years, this will happen." He moved the chalk downward and drew a straight line. As he did so, the chalk hit the tray and broke.

One piece dropped to the floor, rolled toward me, and stopped a few inches from my feet. *This chalk represents my life. I still have some momentum, but soon I will come to a halt.*

A very serious and painful illness had attacked my body—myasthenia gravis, an incurable disease similar to multiple sclerosis and in the same family as Lou Gehrig's disease. I knew money couldn't buy a cure, because multimillionaire Aristotle Onassis, Jackie Kennedy's second husband, died of it.

My muscles deteriorated and became useless. My mouth drooled, and I choked on my own saliva. I couldn't run or do any strenuous activity. Anything that touched my body triggered a shock of pain. My speech became impaired, and breathing laborious. I also suffered from double vision.

My condition forced me to relocate from Argentina to San Francisco, California, for experimental treatments.

Two things kept me going: first, my wife, Ruth, and our four beautiful daughters, ages one through nine; second, the fond memories of Uruguay and Rosario, Argentina, where we came so close to developing a workable model for reaching entire cities for God.

After a thorough and lengthy examination, the San Francisco doctors said, "Mr. Silvoso, we aren't sure we can help you, but you can certainly help us."

As a former hospital administrator, I quickly recognized the true meaning—medical lingo for "Would you agree to become a guinea pig?"

Some procedures were as painful as the illness itself. At one time or another, I received 16 injections a day. That adds up to 480 injections a month. I took 42 pills daily, in addition to 1,500 milligrams of cortisone, and occasional chemotherapy.

Once or twice a week, I was hooked up to a machine that performed a plasmapheresis, a procedure that slowly drained all my blood and disposed of everything except the red and white cells, which were pumped back in. This treatment removed all antibodies from my bloodstream, making me totally vulnerable to infections for forty-eight hours.

I also underwent a thymectomy, in which the surgeon split my sternum bone in two, retracted my rib cage, and removed the tissue underneath. Most discouraging of all was none of these procedures provided a cure but were simply done to keep me alive.

Some nights I grew so weak I believed God was giving me a choice to live or die.

I quickly learned to map the shortest route from my bed to the bathroom. What a difference a few feet made. I stared at the ceiling for hours on end, until I memorized every inch of it.

As hard as it was, Ruth and I resigned from our ministry team to concentrate on whatever time I had left. We focused on devising ways to reach cities for Christ—otherwise, people's eternal destiny would hang in the balance.

One evening I pleaded with God for supernatural guidance. That night I received an immediate answer to prayer through a dream. I saw myself and a group of friends launching a new ministry, Harvest Evangelism. That summer the ministry became a reality. What an exciting occasion!

We began building a retreat center in my native city of San Nicolas, province of Buenos Aires. Within a 100-mile radius, there are more than 109 small cities, towns, and hamlets that have no local churches. I hoped that after I was gone, this retreat center would become a training facility to reach cities for Christ.

In between medical treatments in the United States, I made trips to Argentina to organize and direct the construction of the center. I stayed in Argentina for as long as I was physically able. Upon my return to the States, I crashed at the hospital, feeling very much like Humpty Dumpty, hoping the doctors would be able to put me back together again.

Prayer and medical treatments stretched my initial prognosis past two years, but I barely hung on. My body could quit anytime.

Three years after Harvest Evangelism was born, the San Nicolas chapel and training center were completed and already in use. We dedicated the center to the Lord. A spontaneous explosion of joy filled my heart.

Soon after the dedication, I began to have breakthroughs in my health. In addition, dramatic events began to unfold. A business owner and lay preacher, Carlos Annacondia, held a three-month crusade in La Plata, where 40,000 people made public decisions for Jesus—something totally unheard of at the time.

Annacondia moved on to Mar del Plata, where close to 90,000 people received Christ. From there, he went to San Justo, where almost 70,000 got saved. From then on, a flood of decisions were made as sparks of revival hit city after city.

Imagine this deluge of new converts descending on a church of fifty people. It quickly runs out of everything, from toilet paper to paper cups, folding chairs to Sunday school teachers. Some traditional churches went into shock.

To cope with the growth, church janitors became Sunday school teachers, the Sunday school teachers moved up to superintendents, and the superintendents became associate pastors, and so on. Having heard of our training center, they came to us for help.

These transitions led to an event that dramatically changed my life—an introduction to intercessory prayer. Two friends, Dr. Harvey Lifsey and Mario Gentinetta, challenged me. "Ed, you need to entreat God regarding your illness. Let's set aside three days of intercessory prayer for the sole purpose of finding out whether you are to live or die from this illness."

Our prayer was simple but specific. "If it pleases You Lord, by the third day at bedtime, please make Your will known."

Finally on the third day at midnight, while driving to the center, I asked God, "Are You going to speak to me?" At that moment, the powerful presence of God inundated the car. I began to worship God.

After I parked the car at the training center, the Holy Spirit led me to passages of scripture that spoke to me. I knew God had chosen to heal me through a process rather than instantaneously. My prayer partners confirmed this.

Later I learned spiritual warfare played a key role in my illness. It didn't make sense to me at the time, but the Bible warns: Be on the alert. Your adversary, the devil, prowls around like a roaring lion, seeking someone to devour (1 Peter 5:8).

The following six months I endured the worst period of my illness, but I knew God's promises were being tested by my trials. After that, some elements of my treatment were no longer necessary.

Over a period of time, I was able to discontinue the injections, chemotherapy, cortisone, oral medication, and the plasmapheresis. God overruled my prognosis and completely healed me.

Today I can dance, run around, and do all the things a normal person can do.

My healing has allowed me to serve the Lord in a greater way. In the past three decades, we've seen cities transformed, multitudes come to Christ, and we're now discipling nations. We also put together a free mentoring program on spiritual warfare. Visit: TransformOurWorld.org and click Mentoring for additional information.

The Lord is not slow about His promise, as some count slowness, but is patient toward you, not wishing for any to perish but for all to come to repentance. (2 Peter 3:9)

~ Ed Silvoso
www.HarvestEvan.org

Ed Silvoso, *That None Should Perish* (Regal Books: Gospel Light, 1995), Adapted from chapter 1. Used by permission.

❧ 🕊 ❧

The Christ Painting

During my college days, my friend, a pre-law student, approached me. "Gail, can you help me with a mural of Jesus for the Friday night fellowship group?"

"I've taken art as an elective, but I can't draw. I only know how to paint in the abstract."

"It doesn't matter. Before I came to Christ, I couldn't even draw a straight line, but God gave me a gift. Just make yourself available to the Lord, and He can use you."

After pondering his words, I decided to help.

Soon after, something uncanny happened. The flat winter sunlight streamed through my bedroom windows, giving the room a subtle glow.

It's too cold to get out of bed.

As I lingered in my warm bed facedown on my pillow, a picture of a man appeared through the golden rose flower of my pillowcase. The man's eyes were shut and something bright shone next to him.

I stared at it slacked-jawed. Then it dawned on me, this man looked like Jesus.

We can use this Christ figure for the painting. A very deep peace enveloped me.

I leaped out of bed, grabbed a writing tablet and pencil from my desk, and loped back to my pillow. I tried to sketch the image, but the drawing didn't come close. After a few minutes, I gave up and got ready for school.

When I returned in the evening, I made a beeline to my bedroom and headed straight to my pillow. I gazed at the pillowcase, but the vision of Jesus had vanished.

On another day while studying with my friend in the library, he said, "I had two dreams of the Christ painting. In the first dream, a little Christ figure stood on top of the Mount of Olives. Then a larger image of Jesus appeared in the background, His arms extended out, touching both ends of a large cross. The second dream depicted the close-up details."

My friend, who started painting three days earlier, had already painted the Christ figure by the time I'd showed up to help. "Wow! That's a fantastic image of Jesus." I took a closer look and screamed. "You painted the exact image of Jesus I saw through the flower of my pillowcase!" I paused then noticed the bright thing I had seen was the sunset or sunrise.

My friend pointed to the outer borders. "Paint stained-glass images with objects inside the borders that represent idols."

I stared at him blankly.

© Steven Taira and Gail Kaku

"You know, like money, material things, even sports. They aren't wrong in and of themselves, but when we put them ahead of God, they trap us and become idols in God's eyes."

Giving it deep thought, I painted a stack of books to represent exalting human knowledge over God's. I dipped my brush into the palette and dabbed some acrylic paint on canvas. Then I painted a hand clutching a $100 bill to represent greed. Halfway through the hand, I nearly dropped my brush.

"Oh, no! I accidently painted six fingers." After struggling for some time, I painstakingly fixed it.

My friend said, "The hand is pointing in the wrong direction. It should point toward the Mount of Olives."

I let out an exasperated sigh.

"Gail, surrender your brush to the Lord."

"Uh . . . what?" New to the faith, I was clueless.

"Let the Lord into the painting."

His words didn't make sense to me, but I prayed, "Lord, I surrender my brush to You." I aimlessly slapped paint on top of the old hand, letting out my frustrations. Inexplicably, a perfect hand with five fingers appeared pointing toward the Mount of Olives. I couldn't believe what I saw.

Then I began to help paint the Mount of Olives, and a narrow, straight road miraculously appeared before my eyes. It led upward to the summit where Jesus stood. I gawked.

On the far left side, I dabbed paint on the cliffs, and a wide road supernaturally appeared and led to a dead-end.

Is this what surrendering the brush means? A verse came to mind about the narrow and wide roads. When I returned home, I searched the Bible and found Matthew 7:13–14.

"Enter through the narrow gate, for wide is the gate and *broad is the road* that leads to destruction, and many enter through it. But small is the gate and *narrow the road* that leads to life, and only a few find it. (NIV)

184

Sometime later, I looked up the notes for these verses. Narrow road represents "Believing in Jesus is the only way to heaven, because He alone died for our sins and made us right before God."[1] It also means "diligently striving to follow Him whatever the cost."[2] At the end of our lives, "only our relationship with Christ – our acceptance of Him as Savior and our obedience to Him – will matter."[3]

The broad road is choosing a way other than God's plan, which has eternal consequences. My heart panged with grief, thinking of all the unsaved people on the wide road.

After two months of long evenings and weekends, we completed the painting. Three USC art professors rated the painting as genius. Despite the accolades, my friend very humbly said, "God used our hands, and all the credit goes to Him."

Over time, I had wallet-sized, Christ Cards made from this painting, which I give to people at every opportunity. It's also a tool to help believers talk about their faith. The back of the card contains the ABCs of Christianity and a prayer to receive God's gift of eternal salvation. The cards have been translated into different languages, and each translation contains a website address with resources in that language—Bibles, audio Bibles, video clips, movies, *Father's Love Letter* and more. For a complete listing, visit: majesty.org/jcard

Jesus said to him, "I am the way, the truth, and the life. No one comes to the Father except through Me. (John 14:6 NKJV)

~ Gail Kaku

1-3. The Life Application Study Bible, New International Version edition, copyright 1988, 2005, is published jointly by Tyndale House Publishers, Inc., and Zondervan Publishing House. All rights reserved. Used by permission.

Unwrap the Gift—A Personal Invitation

Our wish is for you to know Jesus Christ intimately and to receive God's priceless gift of eternal salvation. We're each a unique blueprint with a special purpose—our true calling can only be discovered when we fully seek God for His plan.

God made you a very special person and calls you into a personal relationship with Him. He wants to be your best friend.

We all have wrongs in our lives, known as sins, which hinder our relationship with God. To have this barrier removed, we need to put our full trust and faith in God's Son, Jesus, and receive Him as our Lord and Savior. He died an extremely painful death on the cross in our place to pay for our sins.

It's not enough to be a "good" person—we all need the new life God offers us through Jesus and His gift of salvation.

In an interview by Paul Bradshaw with Rick Warren, author of *The Purpose Driven Life,* Rick said:

"People ask me, What is the purpose of life? In a nutshell, I answer, life is preparation for eternity. We were not made to last forever, and God wants us to be with Him in Heaven.

"One day my heart is going to stop, and that will be the end of my body—but not the end of me. I may live 60 to 100 years on earth, but I am going to spend trillions of years in eternity. This is the warm-up act—the dress rehearsal. We were made by God and for God, and until you figure that out, life isn't going to make sense."[1]

Heaven is a real place. God wants to spend eternity with you there. He loves you and has a special plan that only you can fulfill through Him. God, the Father, His Son, Jesus, and the Holy Spirit are one God, known as the Trinity.

You can receive Jesus into your life and begin your personal relationship with Him by applying the following verses:

Acknowledge: For all have sinned and fall short of the glory of God. (Romans 3:23)

Believe: "For God so loved the world, that He gave His only begotten Son, that whoever believes in Him shall not perish, but have eternal life." (John 3:16)

Confess: If you confess with your mouth Jesus *as* Lord, and believe in your heart that God raised Him from the dead, you will be saved. (Romans 10:9)

Apply your faith and recite this prayer in your own words:

Dear Jesus, I turn from my sins and choose to live my life for You. Come into my heart and forgive me for all my sins. Please guide every area of my life and be my Lord and personal Savior. I believe You are the Son of God. You died then rose from the dead for my salvation. From this day forth, I live by faith in a growing relationship with you. Thank You. Amen.

If you prayed this prayer for the first time, we'd like to give you a welcome gift. Visit: kernels-of-hope.com/gift

May you experience a life overflowing with hope!

~ Bob and Gail Kaku

[1] Rick Warren interview is an excerpt from *Decision* magazine, November 2004; ©2004 Billy Graham Evangelistic Association; used by permission, all rights reserved.

Discussion Questions

How can we be a beacon of light to a lost and hurting world? How can we serve people? (John 8:12)

Applicable story: Tebow Time

What are some methods used to break addictions? Describe a time when God corrected you from destructive behavior. (Romans12:1–2; 1 Corinthians 6:19-20)

Applicable stories: Rich and Thin, Break Free, Redeemed

How do we forgive the unforgiveable? Why is it so difficult to forgive? (Matthew 6:14–15; Mark 11:25)

Applicable stories: Edge of the Cliff, Rich and Thin

Why is it important to have church elders or believers pray for healing? Why is fellowship important? (James 5:14)

Applicable stories: Double Jeopardy, Artem, A Calm after the Storm

What positives can we draw from catastrophic events? How do we receive God's love? How do we love Him? (John 15:13–14)

Applicable stories: Hiroshima, Out of the Cataclysm, All Shook Up

Why should we seek God before man? (2 Chronicles 16:12–13)

Applicable stories: When Coping Wasn't Enough, Unstoppable, Artem

How do we build our lives on the rock? Why is that so important? What does sand represent? (Luke 6:46–49)

Applicable stories: Free Fall, One in a Million, Soli Deo Gloria

Why is it so difficult to be a Good Samaritan? How might we change this? (Luke 10:29–37; Psalm 37:3)

Applicable stories: Out of the Tailspin, Angel in Flip-Flops

Note: For Bibles visit: kernels-of-hope.com/discuss

What does *be ready* at all times mean? (Matthew 24:42–44)

Applicable stories: All Shook Up, Out of the Tailspin

How do you feel about "once saved always saved" and how it relates to repentance? (Revelation 2:4–5; 3:15; Luke 13:5)

Applicable stories: One in a Million, Soli Deo Gloria

Describe a time God sent His angels to bring protection. Are some sent in human form? (Psalm 34:7; Judges 13:21)

Applicable stories: Somersault, All Shook Up, Angel in Flip-Flops

Discuss a time you sought God wholeheartedly, and He gave you specific instructions. (Jeremiah 29:11–13)

Applicable story: When Coping Wasn't Enough

Describe a situation where you relied heavily on God. (Psalm 127:1; James 1:5-6)

Applicable stories: Go Tell It on the Mountain, Beyond Limitations, Unfathomable

Why is the blood of Jesus so important? How do we claim this for our lives? (Hebrews 9:22; Ephesians 1:7–8; 1 John 1:9)

Applicable story: Redeemed

What blessings result from obeying God? (Deuteronomy 28:1–2)

Applicable stories: Opportunity Knocks, Go Tell It on the Mountain

Why is it important to befriend both non-believers and believers? (Matthew 28:19–20)

Applicable stories: Out of the Cataclysm, Arms Wide Open, I Was a Kamikaze Pilot

Describe some undeniable acts of God that you witnessed. What impact did it have on you? (Exodus 14:21–22)

Applicable stories: Tea Fire, Make a Difference, How to Stop a Train

How do we balance work with family life? Why is it important to set boundaries? How do we set them? (Matthew 11:30)

Applicable story: A Divine Do-Over

How do we stay strong in Christ? (Joshua 1:8–9; Acts 1:8)

Applicable stories: Korean Hope; There She Is, Miss America; Unstoppable

Why should we honor our parents? (Deuteronomy 5:16)

Applicable stories: A Mirror of My Father, High Flight, Korean Hope

In troubled times, how has God answered specific prayers? Does He understand us? (1 Peter 5:7; Matthew 10:30)

Applicable stories: Cooking Up a Little Faith, Mundaka Ride, How to Stop a Train

How can we cope with the loss of loved ones? What are some ways God comforts people? (2 Corinthians 1:3–4; Isaiah 41:10)

Applicable stories: The Oil of Joy for Mourning, High Flight

Discuss a time God brought you through something very difficult. (Psalm 23:4, 46:1)

Applicable stories: Finding Hope, Unfathomable, Edge of the Cliff

How does Christianity differ from Islam? (John 14:6; 3:16)

Applicable stories: Kamal, Free Fall

How do we cast our cares upon the Lord? Why is prayer of agreement so powerful? (Matthew 18:19–20)

Applicable stories: A Calm after the Storm, Rich and Thin, Unstoppable

Has God ever prompted you to do something? Describe what happened. (1 Thessalonians1:3; 2 Thessalonians 1:11)

Applicable stories: Make a Difference, Edge of the Cliff

Sometimes people who came from a life of crime are strongest in their faith. Why do you think that is? (Mark 2:17)

Applicable stories: The Mob Connection, Redeemed

Describe a time God rescued you. (Psalm 18:19)

Applicable stories: Angel in Flip-Flops, Out of the Tailspin

Why is it important to meditate on God's Word? Why is worship important? (Joshua 1:8; Psalm 1:2; Romans 10:17)

Applicable stories: There She Is, Miss America; Unfathomable

How does Christianity differ from Buddhism? For a free eBooklet visit: kernels-of-hope.com/booklets

Applicable stories: I was a Kamikaze Pilot, A Hard Shell, Opportunity Knocks

What are some ways to control anger? (James 1:19; 3:6)
Applicable stories: A Strum of Harmony, Edge of the Cliff

Why do we need to be born again? (John 3:3)
Applicable stories: A Hard Shell, Soli Deo Gloria, One in a Million

Jesus laid down His life for us and hears us when we cry out to Him in faith. Describe a situation when God heard your cry for help. (Romans 5:8; Hebrews 11:6)
Applicable stories: The Promise, Double Jeopardy, Unfathomable

What does the Bible say about suicide? How can we encourage despondent people? (Matthew 10:28; Job 2:9-10)
Applicable stories: I Was a Kamikaze Pilot, Free Fall, Kamal, Finding Hope

Describe a time when God's words flowed out of your mouth. What are some ways of reaching out to people? (Exodus 4:12; Jeremiah 1:9; Psalm 105:4)
Applicable stories: Arms Wide Open, Edge of the Cliff, The Christ Painting

What were the healing methods used in the following stories? (Exodus 15:26; 1 Peter 2-24; Psalm 107:20; Proverbs 4:20–22)
Applicable stories: Artem; Double Jeopardy; Make a Difference; One in a Million; There She Is, Miss America; Unstoppable; When Coping Wasn't Enough; Finding Hope

What role does spiritual warfare have in healing? How do we put on God's armor? (Ephesians 6:10–18). For free mentoring visit: TransformOurWorld.org and click Mentoring.
Applicable stories: Unstoppable; There She Is, Miss America; Unfathomable

How do we surrender our lives to Christ? What would you say to the person who says all religions lead to heaven? Discuss the wide and narrow roads. (Matthew 7:13–14 NIV; Acts 4:12)
Applicable stories: The Christ Painting, Arms Wide Open

For Bibles and to download Discussion Questions, visit the Kernels of Hope website at: kernels-of-hope.com/discuss

Popcorn Miracles is the first book in the series of inspirational stories that are little "popcorn-sized" reminders of God's nearness. He cares about every aspect of your life from the triumphs to the struggles, both large and small. Each story relates to one of God's many promises in the Father's Love Letter. See excerpt below.

Father's Love Letter

AN INTIMATE MESSAGE FROM GOD TO YOU

The words you are about to experience are true.
They will change your life if you let them.
For they come from the heart of God.
He loves you.
And He is the Father you have been looking for all your life.
This is His love letter to you.

My Child,

You may not know me, but I know everything about you... Ps. 139:1

I know when you sit down and when you rise up... Ps. 139:2

I am familiar with all your ways... Ps. 139:3

Even the very hairs on your head are numbered... Matt. 10:29-31

Discover all of the promises God has awaiting you and begin your journey to receive everything He has in store for you.

Visit: PopcornMiracles.com and check out the comprehensive trailer.

Father's Love Letter excerpt by Barry Adams. Heart Communications Copyright 1999–2012. fathersloveletter.com - Used by permission.